5-19-09

I dedicate this book to my daughter
Caroline and our grandchildren and
especially to my wife Rose who is still
affected by my nightmare from the
past painful memories.

ISBN 1-890461-50-4

Arpad Sardi
His Story

**A Survivor of the
Most Brutal Period
in Hungarian History**

Arpad Sardi
His Story

A Survivor Of The Most Brutal
Period In Hungarian History

Published by: Winlock Publishing Co
26135 Murrieta Road
Sun City, CA 92585
(951) 943-0014
www.winlockgaley.com.

Editorial assistance: Penny Radcliffe and Rev. Hal Lingerman

ISBN 1-890461-50-4

Price: $14.95

Contents

Meditation is the Key

I titled my book "The True Story of a Hungarian Survivor" because it is the story of the dangers and life threatening events which I endured in my youth and from which I survived.

When people asked how I managed to live, I tell them it is not a secret to those who know God and Christ. To those who don't know God, I say, "Seek Him now."

At the worst time in my life I knocked on His door, and He answered. I made a commitment of faith to Him and received Spiritual strength and willpower. My meditations suppressed my agony and Christ Consciousness governed my mind I received the fruits of the Holy Spirit by being faithful and knowing that He would protect me.

My Childhood

I was born in the town of Gyor, in Hungary, on May 26, 1930. My parents had moved to Gyor from the nearby countryside, coming from families that earned their living farming. Usually, the entire family, including children from the age of ten, had to help with the work. My father was drafted into the Army at the age of 21, an involuntary, lifetime commitment. He was a 26 year old soldier when I was born.

In my earliest childhood memory I was standing in my crib, gripping the side rail. My father, in uniform, was standing in front of me talking to me in Hungarian baby talk. Later, in kindergarten, I remember riding a wooden rocking horse, pushing gleefully, enjoying the motion. The nuns, dressed in their Saint Mary uniforms, were watching. I also remember my little sister, two years younger than me.

As time went on, our family moved to Gecse, a small country village of a thousand residents. Later, I learned our move was due to the death of my grandfather Sardi, and my father inheriting his estate. Father kept the farm producing food for the family and part of it to take to the market. The situation allowed him to receive an honorable discharge from the Army. Our adobe house had two bedrooms and a straw roof. There was a clay oven between the two bedrooms with a chimney above it. Economy dictated that we use anything combustible to heat the oven including tree branches, corncob, etc. My mother made the most delicious bread in that oven, three or four loaves at a time. Father would smoke ham, bacon and sausage by suspending them at the top of the oven before lighting it. Having no electricity, we used oil lamps and candles to light our home.

There were two churches in Gecse, Evangelist and Catholic. We were Catholic. All of our family went to church every Sunday where I served as an altar boy. The elementary school was next to the church, and I began my education there when I was seven.

I learned much by participating in village life as a child. My many experiences included the familiar sight of domestic and wild animals, farm products and all sorts of growing things. We had lots of fruit trees and a vineyard at the back of our house as well as cows, horses, pigs, chickens, geese, ducks, a cat and a dog. The dog was so big I could ride on his back. One of my earliest childhood tragedies was when a rabbit hunter carelessly shot my dog in our field. I cried for three days. My heart was broken.

Living on a farm was a lot of fun for me, even though I had to help my parents with their work in our home and in the field. Summer time was best, when I was out of school. I guarded the cows and the geese feeding in the pasture, and I loved watching the jackrabbits cavorting around me, and listening to the birds singing above me. I chased butterflies and mice and climbed an oak tree looking for eggs or baby birds in the nests. I collected butterflies of various colors and sizes, but left the nests untouched. One of our native birds was the stork. They would nest on our chimney top and feed their babies frogs, snakes, mice and anything else that couldn't move fast enough to escape that long hill.

At sunset, I led the flocks of geese and the herd of cows home and my mother milked the cows. I really enjoyed the warm, foamy milk, which mother gave me after straining it through cheese cloth in the kitchen. However, I liked being with father

3

most of the time, helping with food preparation for the animals, plowing, seeding and harvesting wheat, corn and potatoes.

Hungary is a four season country, and winter time brought lots of excitement for me. One of the most exciting times was when father killed a pig for food. On one occasion, it was a cold morning and two foot of snow had fallen during the night. Mother dressed me very warmly, including my winter boots, and I rushed into the back yard and saw father with a neighbor man wrestling a pig to the ground. The pig screamed very loudly for about 30 seconds and then there was silence.

Mother appeared with a big bowl containing some salt, which she used to collect blood from the pig's wounded chest. She later mixed this blood with cooked rice, onions and spices, making sausage with the mixture. When my mother finished catching the blood, I helped my father cover the pig with straw. It provided fuel for a fire that burned off the pig's hair. The fire made the area comfortably warm. I enjoyed pulling off the pig's warm nails and pushing them on to my cold fingertips. Finally, I yanked the roasted tail off and chewed it because it was so good. The taste reminded me of the smell of hickory. Finally, my parents washed and cleaned the animal and my father butchered it.

I stood at the butcher table and watched father working, learning how he reduced the meat to its significant parts; ham, bacon sausage, headcheese, etc. All of these were smoked in the chimney, as I mentioned before, for three weeks. The same methods are still a solid part of tradition in Hungary in the winter, and I feel fortunate to have been able to see and learn about them.

WWII a Safe Haven

I finished the five year elementary school with excellent results. I was 11 years old when my parents registered me in a middle school in the nearby city of Papa. My village to the city was connected by rail, so I could commute to school daily, a ride I enjoyed as well as life at school. I studied 10 subjects at a time, including German. The subjects were mandatory by Government edict. I was obviously occupied with home work, but I didn't mind. I had earned my highest grades in the first two years at the school when a major event affected our family along with the rest of the world. World War II began. My parents gave up farming and because Father was eligible for a Government job, he applied for a job as a prison guard. He was sent to the capitol, Budapest, for a six-month seminar. When he finished there, he got a new uniform, the position he had applied for, and was stationed in the city of Nagykanizsa, close to the borders with Austria and Yugoslavia. My parents sold our previous home and livestock, bought a new house in this city, and soon I was registered in the middle school. There I was, thirteen years old, eager to start new studies at a new school… and there was a war going on.

Before long my father was drafted into the Army. Germany invaded Hungary in 1942 and everyone, including the politicians, had no choice but to give the country up to the German invaders. The politicians had to abdicate their positions to others who supported the invaders. The new politicians aided the Germans, and the Hungarian army joined the German troops in the fight against the Communist Russian army. At this point the battles were taking place in Russian territory. The Germans and their allies had made great advances in battle. After Moscow was struck, the United States entered the war and allied with Russia. This was the turning point in the war.

Russia received the support of military goods shipped from the United States in convoys which crossed the Atlantic Ocean to the Russian Port of Murmansk. American bombers based in England and North Africa began making daylight bombing raids on German supply routes through Hungary. Hungarian cities were subjected to "carpet bombing" on a daily basis. The German army was forced to retreat, slowly at first, from Russian territory with heavy losses of life on both sides. The fight continued on Hungarian fields, and finally the Russian army occupied our country.

My Father was captured by the Russians and taken to Siberia for hard labor. I was 15 by then and my sister, Margaret, and I were still with Mother. Later, we somehow received a message from my father, written on a piece of paper. It said, "I have been captured by the Russians. They carried many of us to Siberia. Pray for us. I love you all. Your Dad." Mother said, "Oh, my God. Oh, my God," crying so hard the tears poured from her eyes. She hugged Margaret and me tightly and we all cried together.

Our city was located near the Western border of Hungary and since the war was still going on we suffered a lot of Russian shelling and attacks by American bombers. In fear for our lives, my mother decided to move away from the city into the country side. In the middle of a forest we found a farmhouse and three families we knew. There was a bomb shelter underneath the house and we all hid there.

Our war-worries continued as the battles advanced toward us. The Russians were driving the Germans westwards and had occupied 95% of our country. They had a very frightening reputation for abusing the civilian population, wantonly raping, robbing and killing innocent people. With the noise of heavy guns, along with explosions that rattled the house above us, and seeing German and Hungarian soldiers retreating in the field, we knew the Russians would soon be coming. Early the next morning, we heard the rumble of the first Russian T-34 tank as it approached our house. We could see it through a slit in the door as it came up the hill, heading toward our house.

It smashed through the fence and gate and stopped before the house. A group of Russian soldiers, who had been following the tank, rushed into the house with machine guns and ordered us out of the shelter. They screamed, "German, German!" and looked for enemy soldiers who might be hiding somewhere in the house or basement. Finding no Germans, they broke all the furniture into kindling, cut up the pillows spreading the feathers all around, and left the area quickly.

There was a bitter fight in the nearby fields, and we saw a hill of dead Russians, killed by the German resistance. As soon as the first wave of Russians rumbled away, another group followed who called themselves the "occupation" force. This was what we had feared. We knew that they would stay in the area for an extended time. They had been given permission to "subdue" the civilian population by ransacking property, raping and killing any person who objected or resisted.

Escaped

It was not long before more of the occupation forces arrived in our area. Many Russians moved in, with horse and buggy rigs loaded with stolen goods. Many were traveling on foot wearing all manner of civilian clothes, including hats normally worn by Hungarian workers, along with their uniforms. Some came on horseback wearing long swords on their belts. They looked more like a gypsy caravan than the Russian army. Most were drunk. We watched through the half open basement door, too scared to expose ourselves or go outdoors.

The door was suddenly kicked wide open and a couple of Russians, with a machine gun rushed in and ordered us out of the basement, forcing us to hold our hands above our heads. One, in an officer's uniform, grabbed a woman from our group and pushed her up the stairs. We later learned that she was raped. A second officer forced the rest of us to go outside and stand in line. It was midnight, totally dark.

He then aimed his loaded pistol at our foreheads, one at a time, saying, "You will all die now, you will all die now", over and over. He was half drunk which made us more scared than ever. My mother and sister were crying, as were the other women.

I was sure that this was the end. I was petrified and thinking very fast when I was struck with an idea. I was next to my mother and when I had a chance, I whispered to her, "I'll run to the officer, hang onto him and beg him not to harm you. When I do, take the chance to run away." She agreed and I immediately ran and jumped on the officer, and loudly begged him not to hurt us. The plan succeeded. I was blocking the officer's view and our group was able to run away.

When he realized what had happened, the officer knocked me to the ground and took off after the group. They had run around to the front of the house and were screaming for help. I joined them, but most of the Russians were drunk and asleep in their wagons.

They were not disturbed by the noise, except for one Ukrainian cook. He awoke and wanted to know what the problem was. The women overcame the language barrier with body language and explained that the Russian officer (pointing at him) was threatening to harm us all. He understood quickly and he assailed the officer first with an argument (which we couldn't understand) and finally he physically attacked him, beating him badly, and chased him away. I found it hard to comprehend how a low-ranking and unarmed cook would dare to, and succeed in, beating an armed two-star officer. We were thankful and felt relief even though our fates remained unpredictable.

Our Ukranian savior wasn't through with us, however. He found a bunch of straw and brought it to us, leading us to the edge of the forest a short distance away. There he placed it in a deep ditch for us to lie down on, protected somewhat from the cold ground. Then he stayed with us all night as a guardian.

It helped, but it was such a cold night that without blankets we suffered terribly from the cold. We nestled together and were able to preserve some heat and kept each other somewhat warm.

Hiding Place

There were seven people in our group. My mother and my 13 year old sister and another woman with two children under ten years old, who were also females. A man named Mike and I were the only males. The woman who had been raped wept continuously. She felt ashamed and could not reconcile her feelings, no matter how much we tried to comfort her. She was blameless and we all felt sorry for her, especially since she had been the first victim and we were all worried about the possibility of being the next one.

Mike had been a prison guard and a friend of my father's before the war, when they served in the army together. The farm and house where we were was actually the property of the Nagykanizsa city prison. Mike had served here as a prison guard, supervising some of the prisoners whose duties were the farm work required to provide food for the prison, mostly farm animals and vegetables.

Mike had knowledge he wanted to share with us; a possible hiding place! He said that when he had prisoners working for him, having realized there was the possibility of Russia taking over Hungary, as well as knowing the reputation the Russian Communists had for avarice and the plunder of subject populations, he had the prisoners modify the pig pens to provide a hiding place in the pig house.

The pig house was made up of three brick-walled rooms with an attic overhead. The attic was accessible through trap doors, one in the ceiling of each room. The normal entrance of each room was a door to the outside. Mike had the prisoners eliminate the door to the central room by bricking it up, leaving no noticeable evidence of the former door. The central room was then accessible only from the other two rooms, and only through the trap doors. The building was left with the appearance of having only two rooms. The third room was to be our hiding place.

There would be no conflict with the animals because, except for one cow, the Russians had already slaughtered them for food, he told us. He also said that there was a small door on one end of the building, near the roof, big enough for a person to get into the attic. The floor of the attic was covered with straw and in the middle of that floor and under the straw was a trap door to the middle room.

"On one end of the building," Mike said, "just below the roof, there's a small door, big enough for a person to get into the attic. In the center of the straw-covered attic, under the straw, there is a trap door which opens to the center room of the pig house. Let's start to move up there, but be very careful. We have to sneak between the sleeping soldiers on the ground without waking them up."

Facing Danger

Mike opened the small door above us and we lifted the children up first, then the two women. My mother was the last and the heaviest. Mike and I had a hard time lifting her up and twice she fell back before we finally got her through the open door.

Soon they found the trap door to the center room and lowered themselves into it, closing the trap door above them. It was total darkness down there. No food, water or sanitation had been prepared ahead of time. Mike and I remained outside after promising the women that we would provide food and water and keep them informed about the outside situation. Mike and I believed we would be safe among the Russians.

The first couple of days went smoothly. I walked back and forth in front of the pig house each day and avoided suspicion. I sent messages to those inside by singing them, and I was able to throw food and water into the attic occasionally.

On the fourth day Mike and I were walking together when we passed the officer who had threatened us with his pistol behind the building that night. He turned suddenly and stopped us.

"Where is your mother?" he asked me.

I pointed my finger toward the city. He knew what I meant. Apparently he was able to understand my body language and he got mad. He grabbed Mike and pushed him toward the house, continuing to push as he followed. I stayed a little distance behind them and after they entered the house I sneaked to a window and carefully looked inside.

I saw the angry officer arguing with Mike, hitting him in the face several times. I could not hear their voices very well, but I figured out that the officer wanted to know where the women were hiding. Mike did not break down. Then I saw the officer pour some kind of liquid into a glass and begin to force Mike to drink it. He resisted, but he was over-powered and finally drank it.

Mike roared in pain, jumping up and down and then ran for the door, yanked it open and ran out. I rushed to him as he doubled over in pain and screamed, "Arpie! Arpie! (my nickname) I'm poisoned! I'm poisoned!".

I knew right away what I have to do and said, "Let's go to the stable. Hurry!" We ran to the stable where there was a cow. I began to milk her hurriedly. As soon as I got enough milk in my container I poured it into Mike's mouth. I continued to milk and pour until he had drunk about a half gallon before he felt better.

"What happened in there?" I asked him.

"He wanted to know where the women were," he answered. "I told him they went back to their homes in the city, but he didn't believe me and got really mad. Then he tortured me by pouring acid and vodka into a glass and forced me to drink it."

It was just as I had thought. At that point I glanced out toward the house and saw the officer heading downhill on his horse. "He's coming after us," I told Mike. "Look!"

"He probably gave up looking for the women. Now he will try to kill us," he said. "We have to defend ourselves. Come on, I have rifles hidden in the bee house. We have to shoot him before he shoots us!"

We ran to the bee house, found the rifles, loaded them and waited. We could see him from our hiding place and were surprised to see him come to a halt. He was half way down the hill and he just sat there looking around. All of the other soldiers were gone and he must have thought we were gone, too, because he turned the horse around and left the farm.

"He must be psychic," Mike said.

He was very lucky because we were ready to shoot him if he had come any closer. We watched him until he rode out of sight, and then we went back to the house to see if everyone was gone. The place was empty. All the furniture was gone. The Russians had burned it to cook their food. They had eaten all the animals except the cow I had milked.

It was very silent now except for cannon and machine gun sounds we could hear in the distance. The war had passed us. Thank God we were saved!

My Father Returns

From Russian Captivity

I ran to the pig house shouting the good news. "All the Russians are gone! There's nothing to worry about, you can come up now."

Mike and I opened the attic door and helped everyone to the ground. They were very pale after spending five days in the small dark room. Too much worry and no exercise had made them shaky on their feet, and mentally and physically exhausted, but otherwise they were relatively healthy.

"We prayed a lot," they said, "and the good Lord listened to us."We all were happy to be together again and hugged and kissed each other, everyone talking at once. We had so much to share about our experiences that we decided to spend one more day at the farm.

The morning of the second day we all decided to go back to our hometown, so we said goodbye to one another, each wishing the other a safe trip, good wishes for their future and promises to pray for each other. We all hoped that we would meet again under better circumstances.

My mother, sister and I had an uneventful trip, and on arrival home we found everything just as we had left it. We missed our father whom we loved very much, but he was still in Russian captivity and we missed having him there to support us financially. We had no money and had to find a way to eat. The only thing we could think of was that we needed something that we could take to other villages and trade it for food.

15

My mother had a wonderful idea. "There is an old oil tanker over on the railroad tracks." she told us, "Let's go over and see if there is anything left in it."

We found that the oil was gone, but in the bottom of the tank there was lots of grease left from the oil. The grease was like a gel and my mother and I spooned it out into a container which we carried to the farmers. They could use the grease on their wagon wheel axels as a lubricant. We traded it for lard, flour, ham, eggs, bread, etc. and continued to do so until it ran out. We had food for awhile, but it was only temporary.

I was sixteen by then and I felt responsible for supporting my family. I wanted to learn a trade. I wanted to be a tool and die maker, so I found a place where I could sign up for a three year apprenticeship. I didn't earn much money, but after one year of experience I was given a promotion and, as a trained person, I earned more money. My workplace was a repair shop owned by the Hungarian-American Oil Company, and I was very fortunate to work for this company because I received a lot of benefits.

After the war, from 1945 through 1947, Hungary suffered greatly from inflation. Because of those whom I worked for, I had free propane gas for the house, and we had discount food from the company store. Elsewhere, there was a huge food shortage. The people had to have food stamps to live on. Besides all of my benefits, our company received relief packages from the U.S.A. and the company distributed them to the employees. I felt so blessed to be working for a company like that.

I would like to mention that my mother had two sisters and a brother living in the U.S.A in South Bend, Indiana. They also were very helpful to us by sending clothing packages and adding dollar bills to their letters. They gave me a good impression of America, and I longed to live there.

My apprenticeship was wonderful and I enjoyed it, but I wanted more education, so I registered in the Commercial and Business Administration College where I took evening classes. My goal was to become a mechanical engineer. It was during this time that my father escaped from captivity.

One night, in 1947, my mother heard a knock on the back door and because it was so late, she looked out a window to see who was there. What she saw there frightened her so much she ran into the bedroom where my sister and I were asleep and woke us. "A long bearded Russian soldier is at the door!" she whispered.

We all walked quietly into the kitchen where we heard the knock again. My mother was afraid to open the door, so she asked, "Who is there? Who is there?"

The answer we heard from the outside was, "Your Dad!" and more loudly "Your Dad!"

My mother cautiously opened the door and there was my father in his original military uniform, the one he was captured in. We all jumped up and down and hugged and kissed him. We were so happy he was home.

My mother instantly discovered he was covered with bugs and took the clothes off him and got the tub ready so that he could clean up. We were so excited that we could hardly wait for him to re-appear. We waited in the bedroom and when he came out of the bath we shouted, "There he is! My Dad! My Dad!!" and we jumped on him and hugged him.

We couldn't sleep and kept asking him questions. We were just so happy to have him with us again. He was very thin and weak from starvation and it took several months before he recovered and was able to go back to his old job as a prison guard.

17

My Passport Denied

I studied hard in school and worked hard in the machine shop. In 1948 I received my Master's Degree as a tool and die maker. Now I was ready to go to college. I took my entrance exam and had no difficulty with it so I was ready to start the next year.

However, fate changed my life and turned me in a different direction. My aunt Irene, who lived in America, sent me an affidavit and an invitation to move to America and stay with her.

I was very excited and surprised by the invitation. I could hardly believe that my dream was coming true. I had to have my parents' approval to get a passport since I was only 18 years old, but my mother didn't want to let me go. I talked to her and told her how important it was to me. I told her I'd send money and that I would return for a visit often.

After much discussion and many tears, she finally gave her permission.I immediately sent an application for a passport to the Hungarian Government and waited anxiously for a response. I could hardly wait to see the mail each day and when the envelope with the passport office return address on it arrived, I jumped up and down with joy. I eagerly ripped the envelope open and began to read. I couldn't believe what it said. I read it again and felt as though I'd been knocked to the ground.

"Your request for a passport is declined. In two years you will be eligible for draft into the army; therefore you may not leave the country." I was so angry and disappointed I felt desperate. All I could think of was how much I wanted to go to America. I felt like someone had knocked me to the ground. There must be a way for me to go.

My sense of urgency was because I had foreseen a bad political situation for Hungary under the Russian occupation. I disliked the Russians. I had experienced many of their barbaric and primitive behaviors during the war. I had seen many innocent people raped, robbed and killed. Russian soldiers would line up and one woman would be raped over and over again. It was happening all over the country and I had witnessed it myself.

I felt that I had good reason to be upset and disappointed with the Russian occupation of Hungary. They brought Communism and terror into my country. Moscow established a leadership, trained in Russia, and put them into Budapest, our capitol. The Russian Army forced us to accept them. By 1949 they took over the Capitol completely by tampering with the election. They then abolished previous coalition parties and jailed their leaders.

Only a few were able to escape to free Western countries. Josef Stalin, the Russian leader, was known to have ordered millions of innocent people killed because they were anti-Communist or good Christians. His atheistic Communist system was a terror wherever he took over a country. Hungary was not an exception.

I lived what I had foreseen in 1948 as it became reality in 1949. I had to make a plan. I had to escape.

I Left Hungary for Austria

I was 18 years old. My passport had been denied. I saw no future in my home country because of my political viewpoint. There was no doubt in my mind that I must get out of Hungary right away. My city was not far from the Austrian border and I made a plan to cross the border and then, once in Austria, I could reach the American zone. I told a friend, Fred, about my plan and asked him if he would like to go with me. Right away he said, "Yes! I'll be happy to go with you. I know we'll have a better future in some Western country."

I took my two week paid vacation from work. I gathered up what I wanted to take with me. It couldn't be much because I did not want to look like I was leaving, especially when we got near the Austrian border. Then I wrote a farewell note to my family.

"Dear Mom, Dad and Sister! I am very sorry to leave like this, but since the government refused to issue my passport, I decided to leave the country illegally. My goal is to go to America. I know it will be a dangerous trip to get across the border and through the Russian zone in Austria, but I have lots of courage and I believe that God will be with me. When I am in a safe place, you will hear from me. Please, please don't cry for me. Just pray and I'll be O.K. LOVE YOU ALL."

I left my letter on the kitchen table, put some sandwiches into my pocket, and left the house. My plan had been to leave when the house was empty so that there would be no one there to try and stop me.

I met with Fred outside and told him, "We can't carry a suitcase. We don't want people to know what we are doing. A suitcase would make them suspicious."

We walked to the train station and bought two tickets. It was about 3:00 p.m. when we got on the train. Two hours later we arrived at the border town of Szombathely, and from there we had to walk down a dirt road to get closer to the border. The sun was getting red on the horizon, and we soon realized that there was a painted bar across the road blocking it. Next to the bar was wooden shed. When we got close, two armed soldiers stepped out of the shed and waited for our arrival. Fred was afraid, but I told him, "Don't worry. Just play cool. I'll do the talking." When we were in front of them I smiled and said, "Good evening, sirs."

"Where are you going? Don't you know this is the Austrian Border?"

"I'm sorry," I said, "We have no intention of crossing the Border. We are looking for a village (which I named), would you be kind enough to tell us which direction we must go to find it?"

"We don't have any idea," one said, "but one thing I can tell you is that you better go back before you get into trouble."

"Thank you very much. We surely don't want to come this way again. Have a nice evening, sir," I said, and we turned around to go back.

Soon the road turned 90 degrees and the soldiers could no longer see us.. We were lucky they hadn't arrested us, but I had convinced them that we were not refugees.There was a small forest along the road here and beyond it an open field. We decided to take shelter in the forest until midnight, now that we knew where the border was. When we did start across the field, which was very dark, we carefully made our way until we suddenly stumbled onto a deep, wide ditch. We were pretty sure that it was the border, so we quickly and quietly made our way down the one side, hurried across the ditch and up the other side where we broke into a run, excited with the knowledge that we were running on Austrian soil.

We didn't encounter any guards or soldiers and soon we saw the lights of a village about two miles away. We immediately turned and headed in that direction. As we reached the outskirts and approached the first house we saw, in its backyard was a huge stack of straw. We had been walking for two hours and were very tired so we decided to dig a hole in the straw and crawl in and sleep.

It was daylight when we woke up, which frightened us a bit because if someone noticed us and reported us to the authorities, we could be deported back to Hungary. We had to hide because this part of Austria had been in the Russian Zone since the war ended. We had to be careful to avoid contact with the police, Russian soldiers and even civilians who might be agents for the Communist Authority.

We must have slept well because when I pulled myself out of the straw the sun was brightly shining in my face, which made me nervous. We should have been on the road a long time ago crossing the field that would take us toward the West and the English Zone. I knocked on Fred's side, while he was still sound asleep. I shook him and said, "Let's go, Fred, hurry and get up before the farmer finds us here. We can't waste any time."

We left in a hurry and spent the day wandering across pastures, through woods, and up and down hills. Sometimes we rested a little bit. We had eaten the sandwiches I brought from Hungary earlier and now we were hungry and thirsty, but we kept on going west. Late in the afternoon we knew we were very close to the Russian-English Border when we were fortunate enough to meet an Austrian farmer in his field and asked him about the border situation.

He was very friendly and pointing his finger he said, "Out there is a small river. If you cross it you will be in the English Zone and be safe. But you have to watch out for the Russian Border patrols. Good luck and God bless you."

As we moved quickly in the direction he had pointed out, I was thinking how grateful I was that he had spoken German. I was fluent in German and I was not only able to understand him, but I was able to thank him, too.

It was sundown when we got to the river. We did not see any Border patrol. What I did see was a steel wire fastened in the water and I realized it was a triggering device to an alarm system for the Russian Border post. We couldn't take the risk of swimming across the narrow river, but the branches of a big tree on the other side were there for our rescue. They bent all the way to our side of the river giving us the ability to reach one and bend it down to the ground. The branches formed a bridge that allowed us to crawl over to the other side. I went first. and Fred followed. We danced with happiness – we were in the English Zone!

We ran for a while in the darkness away from the Border, always going west. Eventually, we saw a small village lit up in the distance, so we went toward it. I knew we didn't have to run any more, so we decided to report into the police station and ask for political asylum.

We reached the outskirts of the town, and as we walked down the street we saw two gendarmes coming toward us. Just whom we wanted to see! When they got closer, I said in German, "We'd like to report to the station. We are refugees from Hungary."

"Let's go," they answered, and escorted us to the station.

The commander, who was sitting behind his desk, welcomed us. He was very polite, and after we showed him our I.D. he began to type the report. "Why did you leave your home?" he asked.

"I don't like the Russians," I answered. They brought Communism to the country and forced people to join the Communist Party. I didn't want any part in it. My idealism doesn't agree with theirs. I'd like to go to America where I have relatives waiting for me." Then I showed him the affidavit my aunt had sent me.

He asked Fred the same question and Fred expressed his antipathy toward Communism also. After the commander finished his report he gave us food and blankets, and told us, "You have to go down to the basement to spend the night. Have a good sleep and tomorrow we'll escort you to a refugee camp in another city."

We were very tired and hungry. After we finished our sandwiches we fell asleep in the basement. Actually, we slept in a jail cell behind bars. It was a scary situation, but our exhaustion knocked us into a deep sleep.

We awoke to the sound of a genarme yelling, "Wake up! We have to go!"

We gathered our few belongings and folowed the man upstairs. The commander was waiting there. He shook our hands, as he wished us good luck, and two other gendarmes escorted us to the railway. The train was just pulling in and they saw to it that we boarded it. I didn't have any idea where we were heading, but after a three hour trip, we pulled into a station which had the name, "Leibnitz" on the wall.

Leibnitz was located in the Southern part of Austria, close to the Italian border. From the station we were escorted to a refugee camp. It was in a large brick building which had served as an Austrian military barracks during the war. We found many refugees there.

Some had served in the military during the war, and others who had left Hungary the year before for the same reason that Fred and I had.

The conditions in the barracks were terrible. The food supply, as well as the sanitation, was beyond belief. It turned out that the barracks were a slave trade center. Austrian farmers visited every day looking for young, strong males for their farm work. They offered no pay, only food and shelter. Because of starvation in the barracks many men went for the opportunity to have food.

French Foreign Legion recruiters also came and offered the young men a brilliant life and a joyful future. In fact, my friend, Fred, became convinced and signed up. It was a heart-breaking moment when we had to part. He was a good companion on our journey. Now I felt lonely and restless, but I had to consider my own fate. The first thing I had to do was write to my aunt in America, tell her where I was, and ask her for money. I needed it to help me buy a document and have some left for food.

In two weeks her answer arrived. Enclosed was a $20 bill. I was very happy and immediately put the money into a secret pocket of my jacket to make it difficult to be stolen. In the letter my aunt wished me good luck and told me she was worried about me.

I wrote back immediately and expressed my appreciation for the money and for her concern for me. I also told her that now I would find out how to get to the American Zone in Salzburg, and get to the American Embassy where I hoped to pave my way to America.

Travel to Salzburg

I decided to leave the barracks illegally. I couldn't leave through the gate because it was guarded. It seemed that the only chance I had was to climb up the brick wall which surrounded the place and drop over the other side into the street. I had a plan, and early in the morning I executed it. I was a free man again.

I walked to town and mailed my letter. The second part of the plan was to exchange my $20 for Austrian shillings. As I walked down the street, several Jews surrounded me and tried to sell me American gum, cigarettes and chocolates. They asked me if I had any jewels or dollars. When I said I had some dollars they became very excited, and offered me an exchange at black market prices. Their first offer of 30 shillings per dollar did not sound good to me, so I started to walk away. They followed me and kept offering me different prices. When they offered 40 shillings per dollar I agreed. I watched as they counted 800 shillings into the palm of my hand. I was happy and they were, too.

After I got my shillings I still had to get the I.D. that would enable me to travel in the country, but I knew where to get it. I had to get to the city of Linz. I bought a train ticket, taking a chance that nobody would stop me on the way. I was lucky. There were people all around me on the train, and I chatted with them. I enjoyed the spectacle of nature through the train's windows. We were passing through green pastures and woods, and everything was bright and sunny.

I got a little homesick thinking of my parents, my sister and

27

my motherland, but I overcame it by keeping my mind focused on the purpose of my journey. Time goes by fast when your mind is occupied. The train had stopped. I looked out the window and saw the station's building with a big sign on it – Linz. "This is the town," I told myself. I left the train with the rest of the people and walked with them out to the street..

The city was completely unknown to me, but I could speak the language. As I walked down the street I walked up to a man who appeared friendly and asked "Where can I find the passport office?"

"Not too far," he replied, "Go to the second street and turn right. You can't miss it." He pointed down the street as he continued. It's a tall gray building and on the third floor there's a sign that says "Passport Office."

After I thanked him for his kindness I found the place on the third floor and the time of day was perfect. A man greeted me immediately and asked, What can I do for you?"

I spoke to him in a German language called "Fier Sprache Auswise." I would like to get an I.D." I told him.

"No problem," he said. He then took my picture and in a couple of minutes my document was done. It looked like a passport with my name, nationality and photo on it. It had been written in four languages; German, English, Russian and French. That was just what I wanted. I was happy to pay him 120 shillings for it. I could now travel without fear in Austria.

After I left the office I realized I was very hungry, so I found a nice restaurant to eat in. Money was no problem and I ordered the best meal on the menu with a mug of good beer. My dinner was perfect, and my stomach was happy. When I left the restaurant, I walked back to the railway station and bought a ticket to Salzburg, which was the city in which the American Military Headquarters of the Counter Intelligence Corps (CIA) and the International Refugee Organization (IRO) were. The IRO building, where several free nation Consulates had offices, was where I wanted to go to. That's where the American Consulate was, and I was eager to seek their help.

After I bought the ticket, I had a two hour wait for the train and decided it was a good opportunity to sit in the waiting room and write a postcard to my parents.

"Dear Mom and Dad,

I'm fine. Don't worry about me. Right now I'm in the Linz railway station waiting for a train to take me to Salzburg where the American Consulate is. Aunt Irene sent me money to live on, so I'm not starving either. As soon as I get to Salzburg I'll write again with the result of my trip.

LOVE TO YOU ALL, your son, Arpi"

Not long after I dropped the card into a mailbox, my train arrived. It was late evening in the month of June, 1948, a beautiful, warm evening, when I got on the train. I had purchased a first class ticket for a comfortable, long ride to Salzburg and settled in. As we rode along, I became acquainted with some Austrian citizens and as we chatted I told them my life story, including my adventures and my destination.

They had so many questions that we talked and talked and the time just flew by. The next thing we knew, we had arrived at Salzburg. They were very kind and friendly and wished me good luck as we parted.

I stepped off the train at 3:00 a.m., and suddenly I felt lonely again. Once again I was in a place I'd never been before. I was fortunate that I knew the German language, so I knew I wouldn't get lost. I went through the station and out into the street, which was deserted at this time of night. I looked around to see if there was a hotel. I saw one sign that was still visible. It said "Hotel Europe," but it had been half destroyed during the war and was in shambles. About a block away I saw a barrack built out of wood. When I got closer I could see it was a refugee camp, built after the war, and it had some inhabitants. I wondered if I could stay there until the sun rose in the morning when I could search for a decent hotel close by. As I entered the first building, a man appeared and in Hungarian asked me, "What are you doing here?"

I was startled by his sudden appearance and the fact that he spoke my native language."I'm also Hungarian!," I asked him, "I was hoping I could stay here until daylight."

"Sure!" he replied.

We were friends immediately, and he led me to a room where I could sleep. I slept for about three hours while the moring sunshine came through the window, hitting my face. I got up and looked for the man who had helped me. After I found him, it turned out he was the manager of the camp and and has a little café at its entry.

He invited me for breakfast, which I gladly accepted, and then we chatted. He told me that the population of the camp was mostly Hungarian and that they had been there since the war's end, waiting their transportation to another free country. I told him that it was my purpose, too. then I asked him, if he knew of any hotels nearby I could stay in.

"Yes," he said, "not too far from here in the Stauffen Strasse you will see a hotel. It is not very expensive either."

I thanked him for everything again and promised to visit him again. Then we parted. It was a short distance to the hotel, as he had told me. I don't remember the name, but it satisfied my needs. The room I was shown wasn't fancy, but it had a decent bed and a bathroom with a shower. "Now I can get a goodnight's sleep," I told myself, "and a good shower for the first time since I came to Austria."

Seek VISA for USA

It was June 30th, 1948. I sat in my hotel room and wrote a letter to my Aunt Irene. I told her about my arrival in Salzburg and that I was in good health so far. I gave her my hotel address and assured her that I would stay there while I managed my fate. I would do everything I could to get my visa to America, and as soon as I knew anything I would send her a telegram.

The next day I went to the American Consulate's office and talked to a representative there. I showed him the affidavit from my aunt and told him I wanted to go and live in America.

"I'm so sorry to tell you this," he said, "but the American government has no quota for immigrants at the present time, and won't have for at least a couple more years. I know this is bad news, but I can't do anything about it. You might be able to go to a number of other free countries, such as South American countries, New Zealand, Australia, Canada, and so on."

I was shocked. I didn't know what to say. I choked and almost cried. After a pause I took a breath and said in a low tone, "Thank you," and left the office. I was very depressed. I took a city bus to my hotel and threw myself on the bed. I was very disappointed in the American government, the only ones who closed the door and would not let the refugees in.

After the war, all over Western Europe, and mainly in Germany, thousands of refugees of many nationalities were waiting to get into the U.S.A. Then in 1950 it got worse. I didn't want to go to any country other than the U.S.A. and I felt very uncomfortable about staying in Austria for two more years. I didn't know what to do next. I was 18 years old without much life experience. I felt that I needed advice from someone.

Next morning, as I walked to the lobby, I met a group of distinguished looking Hungarians. I introduced myself to them and found out that they were various party leaders and that some of them were veteran military officers now in exile in Austria's American Zone. They were staying in this hotel. I felt they would understand what I was going through so I told them where I was from and why I was in Austria. I told them about my disappointment, my desolation and concern because of what the American Ambassador had told me. They were very sympathetic and offered some consolation and suggested that we get together after their meeting the next morning. I could hardly wait and wondered what they might suggest to me.

After a sleepless night, I watched the sunshine as it broke through the bedroom window. It was beautiful, and it filled me with hope and optimism about my future. I was eager to meet with those people again, so I dressed and hurried down to the dining room where I found them around the breakfast table. When they saw me, they signaled me to join them and ordered breakfast for me.

Their conversation was on the fate of the Hungarian political situation, and I just listened and waited to see if they would involve me in their politics. They told me there was a movement going on; a military plan to liberate Hungary from Communism. They would try to recruit an army from thousands of refugees. The planning was already done, and the papers had been turned over to the American government and the Pentagon for ratification. The plan requested support for the Hungarian Liberation Army by sending American military surplus supplies and weapons. These organizers were highly educated, intelligent and experienced leaders, both militarily and politically.

"Arpad, we need you in the military. We will make preparations for your position in the armed forces. You can't go to America now so we would like you to stay with us and work to liberate our country. First, we would like to put you into the Intelligence Service. We'll get you back to Hungary on a safe route so you will not have to worry about being caught at the border. When you get to Hungary, we will contact you by letter, which will be written in code. It will sound like just a friendly letter, but each word will ask you about whatever information we are interested in. You will reply in the same way. We will let you know when you are finished with your task and bring you back to Austria the same way we took you out. We will train you in everything before you go, which will take about a week. If you fulfill your service successfully, it will be your first glory to your country and the first steps in your career."

They convinced me. I loved my country and I was ready to fight against Communism at any time. I saw a very promising future. I had to give up the idea of going to America, so I wrote another letter to my aunt. I told her about what the ambassador said about my visa and how disappointed I was, which was followed by a deep desolation.

"I don't want to stay in Austria for two more years," I wrote her, "and I don't want to immigrate to any other country, so I've decided to go back to Hungary. Maybe I will wait a couple of years and try again. Thank you to everyone who supported me financially. I promise I will write to you when I get home again."

With love , Arpi.

Disappointment & Later

I had a new dream now. I wanted to be a hero, a freedom fighter. I wanted to liberate my country from Communism. I liked the idea. The feelings for my homeland gave me a new challenge... the possibility to reunite Hungary. I never thought I would become involved in politics, but my nationality just rose up in me, and I was ready to go back to Hungary and fight.

One man from the group (an opposition party leader in the Coalition Government in Hungry until 1948) took care of me, gave me instructions and prepared me for my journey back home. He escorted me to the railway station and wished me good luck. The only luggage I had was a little backpack with some food in it. It was late evening when I arrived in Vienna. A man was waiting for me at the station and took me to his residence where I would spend the night. The residence was a room in a tavern; it was sort of a hiding place. I guessed he was a smuggler on the espionage route, but I didn't care. I even got a good night's sleep on the floor.

He woke me at dawn and took me to the Austrian/Hungarian border where he handed me over to another man. The second man showed me the exact place in a field where I could cross over the border safely. I followed his instructions and didn't have any trouble or see any border patrols. I ended up in a near-by Hungarian village railway station where I saw several border guards and workers. The workers were evidently going to work in a nearby city. I got a bit nervous about the guards, but I mingled with the workers, pretending I was part of their group. The guards didn't bother the workers about I.D. cards, so I was safe with them and got on the train without difficulty. My destination was only 60 miles away, and the train soon arrived there. As I got off, I made the decision to visit the town where my mother was born. It was on my travel route and only three miles away. Some of my mother's relatives still lived there, and I walked on the same road that I had walked as a child to reach their home. It seemed much shorter now.

My relatives were very happy to see me and greeted me with great hospitality. I stayed with them for a week. I sent my parents a postcard to let them know where I was. My mother responded with happy tears and took the first train available to come and take me home. It was a tearful reunion when she arrived and she said, "I'll not let you loose from me again."

When we arrived home, my father hugged me and said, "You really gave me a headache, son. Now I must go to the police station and report your return because you have been filed as a missing child." He went the next day and told them the good news. They knew my father as a prison guard at the facility located right behind the station, so they handled my case as "just another teen-age adventure."

I kept my Austrian assignment secret from everyone, including my parents, but I did tell them that I was acquainted with some people there who had become my good friends and I would be exchanging letters with them.

I got my old job back at the Hungarian-American Oil Company as a tool and die maker. I started school in the evenings studying business administration. I was very busy and tired, but never so tired I stopped thinking about the politics and the future of my country. As we entered the year of 1949, Hungary geared up for the presidential election.

The Communist Party, backed by the Russian Army, did everything they could to win. They forced people to join the Communist Party, which left Hungary without an Opposition Party because the Party leaders had been jailed. Only the Social Democratic Party existed, but it was forced to convert to the Communist Party. The Hungarian people tried to resist the Communists, but anyone who spoke against them was arrested by the Secret Police, under the direct command of the Russian K.G.B. (Russian Gestapo).

I saw the invasion of the K.G.B.* Terror and dictatorship ruled Hungary. People lost their freedom totally. Criticizing was out of the question. The only newspaper allowed was a Communist one. If anyone tried to speak against the Communists they paid with a minimum five year sentence in prison, if they were lucky and not to be beaten to death before they were put behind bars.

Farmers lost their fields as they were forced to join the (Russian style 'kolkhoz') collective farm. Churches were attacked and their leaders were jailed or executed. People who had the courage to go to church were arrested for sympathizing with the so called "Clerical Black Reactionaries." They were named for the color of the priest's uniform.

The courageous Catholic Cardinal Josef Mindszenty, who raised his fearless voice against the Communist/atheist ideology and encouraged millions to resist, was arrested. He became a sample and hero of the Hungarian people. His followers, as well as many priests, were persecuted, tortured, or beaten to death.

Borders were sealed, especially on the west side, by a double row of barbed wire fencing with mines planted between the

* K.G.B. Intelligent, Counter-intelligent, and Secret Police
Agency of the former Soviet Russia during the Stalin Era.

rows. Towers were built complete with machine guns and reflectors, which soon became known as "the iron curtain." The Russian K.G.B. put together a replica of itself in Hungary as an organization called A.V.H* ., which stood for "National Security Forces." This force was made up of their most trusted Hungarian Communists who operated secretly in civilian clothes. Some were also put into specially designed uniforms, like army uniforms. The ones who dressed in civilian clothes were the detectives and Nazi hunters who arrested thousands and thousands of innocent people, dragged them into custody where they disappeared and were never seen by their families again.

People were hurt and cried out. They demonstrated and got very angry, but people who worked in factories were afraid to talk to the person they worked next to because they were never sure if that person was an undercover agent of the A.V.H. The usual pattern was to have every third person as a "fink" or spy. Many people were forced to be a fink. Those who tried to resist got beaten or a member of their family was held as hostage until they signed the contract and became a fink. The A.V.H. was the top authority, even above the Communist Party or the government. They were the "God" of life and death.

Several underground movements, resistances, occurred in Hungary at that time under different names in different parts of the country. People listened to foreign radio broadcasts like the BBC from London, the Voice of America from Washington D.C., and the most aggressive one, Radio Free Europe from Munich, Germany. All were broadcasting news in the Hungarian language. Radio Free Europe, which people listened to the most, constantly encouraged resistance against Communism and assured the people that the free Western world would help, when we needed their help, to gain back and secure our freedom. Eisenhower, before he became U.S, President, declared, "I will

* A.V.H. Intelligent Secret Police Aganccy of Hungary (1945-1956)

be behind, and support all these people who are suffering when they rise against Communist terrorism behind the "iron curtain". The Hungarian people were happy to hear those words and it helped them to create more conspiracies and more intensive underground movements.

Underground Activity

I felt it was time for me to act. I had five close friends about my age and I asked them if they would like to join me in anti-Communist activity. They agreed, so I laid out my plan to make anti-Communist leaflets and pass them out to people. I took the lead as the mastermind. I wrote the texts, but I didn't have a copy machine. I looked in a school storage room, and found an old broken one. I took it home and fixed it so that it worked well enough for me to copy hundreds of leaflets. The most dangerous work was the distribution of them. The six of us had a meeting and carefully worked out how we could do it.

At night, when very few people were on the street, we all went to work. We stuck those leaflets on almost every street sign, on the walls of houses, and on electric poles all over the city. The next morning thousands of people read them and put them in their pockets. We watched from a distance and were very satisfied with the result of our work.

That was only the beginning. I made more and more with different wording and we distributed them. I made contact with people in various villages in the Province where my leaflets had a huge impact. Not only did the people receive spiritual strength, but strength for more resistance. The leaflets were like hot pepper up the Communists' nose.

The A.V.H. was put on full alert. Their secret agents virtually invaded the whole province looking for suspects. Spies were everywhere. Residences were spot checked without search warrants. Homes were stormed, and everything in them was turned upside down while the Agents looked for evidence on where the leaflets were coming from.

In spite of their actions, I didn't stop my anti-Communist activity. I printed more and more leaflets, which were left everywhere. Meanwhile, I sent information about my activities to my friends in Switzerland and told them what was going on in Hungary politically and militarily. It was nothing but terror in Hungary after Hungary became a "satellite country" of Russia headed by Josef Stalin.

Christmas, 1949, was a sad one. Everyone was afraid to celebrate. The windows in nearly every house in town were dark. Inside the houses Christmas carols were sung softly and carefully so that no one outside could hear them. Communist spies were everywhere. It was a nightmare. The A.V.H. picked people up every night, and some were never seen again. Nobody knew who the next victim would be. All we heard was constant terrorism. Loud speakers were installed all over the city roaring Communist slogans and songs all day and all night. Giant lit red stars were installed on the tallest buildings. Stalin's portraits were all over the city, even in the schools. There was a corner, called "Red Corner," where an enlargement of Stalin's picture was placed. Students were forced to worship him.

It was a crime for anyone even to mention the word "God." For the little children they built a vending machine, which dropped candy out after the children praised Stalin, as their father, as their god. Parents were afraid to correct the children at home, because the child might mistakenly tell on them at school, and the A.V.H. might hear of it.

It was also risky to have a radio. If someone had a radio capable of tuning into Radio Free Europe and it was discovered, the radio was confiscated, the owner prosecuted and beaten as

41

well as being tagged as an "American imperialist sympathizer."

December 27, 1949: Stalin's birthday. Hungarians called it the shortest and darkest day of the year. The Communists prepared a huge celebration in every city and village in the country. The forest of red flags with giant pictures of Stalin, like a tidal, wave ran down the streets. The loudspeakers burst the air with Communist propaganda and music. Factory workers had been forced out into the street to carry the flag poles and Stalin's Portraits.

My friends and I had also prepared for this big event. I printed as many leaflets as I could. Whatever I knew about Stalin, I printed on the paper. I called him an anarchist, a notorious number one killer and monster. "He has millions of innocent peoples' blood drying on his cruel hands." I told that he was also a train robber who stole a large amount of the people's money from the money carrier train. Stalin was the devil himself in human form. I said here he is now, the greatest leader of the big Soviet Union, stretching his bloody hands over our country to kill you if you do not smile and clap to his picture and him. "We have to celebrate this devil's birthday today? Never! Never! Never accept this evil in your heart."

I said all these things and much more. That night before the big celebration began, we placed those leaflets all over the city and the countryside. We tore down all the red flags and materials from the walls and posts in the city. In the morning before the celebration was to start the whole city looked like a disaster – like a tornado had struck. The officials were very angry and had to delay the demonstration for half a day in order to repair all the damages.

Arrest

A dditional A.V.H. was called in, and so many agents arrived that they practically invaded the whole province as they made very intensive searches for suspects. We were lucky that none of us were caught in the action, even though I had organized the countryside already. We had about 200 members.

On the first of January, I received a letter from Switzerland. The friend I had been corresponding with told me a shocking story about the outcome of their efforts to organize the army which would liberate Hungary from the Communist yoke. The immigrant military officers sent their plan to the American government for approval, but the American government not only rejected the idea, saying that Hungary was not of vital interest for them to support such an idea, but they sent Nazi hunters and C.I.A agents to arrest the immigrant leaders who had any connection to the Hungarian freedom fight.

He said, "The C.I.A. tried to arrest us and deport us to the A.V.H. in Hungary. I'm sorry I have to write this; but we had to escape from Austria to save our lives. If you are interested in going back to Austria, we can still provide a safe way out of Hungary. Otherwise, your mission is over. Let us know your decision." The whole letter was written in the "flower language" – our code.

I was very disappointed with America's response, but I knew that the "blockers" were those who ruled the whole world with their power. I knew that I couldn't go on with my political activity too much longer. Sooner or later the A.V.H. would catch me and kill me, so I decided to leave the country. I told my buddies about it, and they wanted to go with me. I started to destroy all the evidence of my activities starting with the copy machine. I dumped it in the ditch on the outskirts of the city. I was in the clean up process every day when one night something tragic happened to me.

On the tenth of January my father was on duty at the prison. My mother, my sister and her boyfriend and I visited some friends in a nearby village. It was a very cold night when we returned home, even the house was cold. I started a fire in the fireplace, but smoke blew into the room so I opened a window to get it out. My mother got into bed to get warm and the rest of us huddled in front of the fireplace to get warm. As we chatted we heard a noise outside. I looked out the window and saw a station wagon stop in front of the house; three men got out. One of them was my father in his uniform, the other two were dressed in civilian clothes, and as they approached the front gate, one of the men ran and jumped through the open window and drew a pistol on us. My father and the other guy came in the door. I did not have any idea what was going on and I asked my father what happened to him. One of the guys quickly asked my father which one of us was his son and before he could answer I said, "I am."

Both of the men grabbed me by the arms and dragged me out into the back yard where they beat me with their fists. I knew I was in trouble and in the hands of the A.V.H., but I didn't know who reported me. The men twisted my arms behind my back and pushed me back into the house and made me show them my room They took everything they could and stuffed it into a bed sheet, which they put into the car with my father and me. On our way to the police station, they went by the prison and let my father out so he could go back to work. Then they took me to the second floor of the police station to interrogate me.

I was the only one arrested so far, and I knew I was in trouble because all the evidence was in their hands, and as soon as they opened the steel box they brought from my room the contents would speak for themselves. The box held all the original copies of my leaflets, the names and addresses of my five friends and the letters I had received from Switzerland.

I had to stand against the wall with my hands behind my back while the two detectives searched the items which they had packed in the bed sheet. The first item was the steel box. It was locked and they asked me to open it up. I had the key in my pocket and I gave it to them. When they opened it they shouted, "Jackpot! We've got them!" They then sat me at their table and asked me who my boss was.

"No one," I answered.

"Who are these guys?" they asked, pointing at the paper with the names.

"Those are my friends." I replied.

"Conspiracy!!" they shouted and ordered me back to the wall again, but this time I was forced to stand about 12-15 inches away from it, facing it with my hands behind my back and leaning my forehead against it so that I was standing at an angle with my forehead holding my weight. One detective left and the other one watched over me. Three hours later the first officer returned with all five of my friends. They had been taken from their beds and brought in. They were then made to stand facing the wall just as I was.

The detective asked each of them the same questions, "Who is your boss? Who wrote the leaflets and had you distribute them?"

Of course, my friends answered the same as I did, "No one."

Both of the detectives got very mad and started to kick us and beat us with a rubber stick until we fell on the floor screaming in pain. Finally, I told them, "I'm the one who wrote the leaflets and copied them with an old copy machine. I broke that machine and dumped it into a ditch at the cemetery."

They didn't buy my story. They didn't think I was intelligent enough to create such a concept as the leaflets. They didn't give up their belief that some grownup, intelligent person was behind our activities. They started with me again.

They made me sit at a table with a variable voltage generator on it. They demanded that I put my hand on a copper pad and when I did they clamped my hands to it. Again they asked me, "Who is your boss?"

"No one," I answered.

"Oh, no?" they shouted and cranked up the voltage on the generator. I felt a great shock and a sudden pain in my arm which went numb. It was a terrible feeling.

"Well," they said, "will you tell us who your boss is?"

"I told you, nobody!"

They gave me another, but higher voltage shock and I passed out. They poured water on me and when I regained consciousness I told them, "I can prove that I'm the only one who wrote the leaflets. I can write, word for word, exactly how they are done."

"O.K." they shouted, and tossed a piece of paper to me. I

wrote every word of every leaflet and they were astonished when I was done, but I had finally convinced them.

Brought to Court

I felt victorious and I thought that I would avoid further interrogation. That was what I thought, but there was another matter – my Austrian and Switzerland connection. Those letters, on the surface, were not anything other than friendly letters, free from any illegal political information. They interrogated my friends about them, but all five of them knew nothing about my connection with the free world. In spite of that the detectives roughed them up, trying to get information. They finally decided to overlook the letters and made preparations to take us to court where we would be told our punishment. Meanwhile, we were locked in the police station's basement cells.

My parents knew where we were, so my mother got a permit to bring us some food. My friend's parents did also. We were very hungry as well as physically beaten. We shared each parent's basket and ate very fast.

I found a note in my mother's food basket. She wrote, "I found out who your informant is. It doesn't matter how. His name is Leslie Kiss. Do you remember when he was a student two years ago and lived with us one year? Now you can figure out for yourself how he could be the man who informed on you."

Yes, I remembered him. He was a good friend then. When he finished school he went back to his country village and I didn't hear about him until 1949. We accidentally bumped into each other on the street in my hometown. We were happy to meet again and we talked about our time in school together and when he lived in my home, and so on. Then he told me he was the President of the Democratic Youth Organization. He wanted me to join them.

"I don't belong to any organization, and I don't want to in the future either." I told him. "I hate Coommunists and their idealism."

It seemed as though he didn't like my attitude, but we wished each other good luck, shook hands and parted. That was the last time I saw him.

As I have said, many secret agents had invaded our town. They watched people as they walked the streets either alone or in groups. The agents would walk behind them and listen to their conversations in their search for suspects. They had a meeting with the youth organization and called their attention to the underground movement and the conspiracy against the current political system. The youths were told, "That movement is active in this province and in this city right now. If you know of any suspicious individuals, report to us right away."

I'm sure Leslie Kiss thought that here was a way to earn a medal by reporting me as a suspect. He knew my father was a local prison guard, and the agents could pick him up by force from work and make him show them where he lived. Finally it became clear why he was with them when they stormed our house without a warrant. I had thought it was my father who was in trouble. It was a routine blind checkup from a tip to the AVH agents, and they hit the jackpot.

Later, when I was in prison, I had a chance to talk to my mother for five minutes. She told me that she had met with my informant in his office. She was very angry and she asked him, "Why did you report my son as a suspect to the AVH?"

He didn't deny anything. He answered, "I did it for merit."

My mother cursed him as she left, and we found out later that her curse came true. He had lost his eyesight.

The AVH agents, who interrogated us and documented the charges against all six of us, sent the documents to the court, which was in a city in another province. The court was a special one which dealt with political cases under the control of the AVH only. They were the highest power over life and death.

The charges were underground cónspiracy, undermining the Communist Government system, and showering people with leaflets which encouraged greater resistance against the ruling government. I was also charged with illegally crossing the border twice, corresponding with people in Switzerland who sympathized with American imperialism, and I was possibly a spy for them.

They chained the six of us together and, guarded by two armed, uniformed policemen, we walked through the city to the railway station. It was very cold and snowy, and we were wearing the light clothes we had on when we were arrested. We arrived at the station where the people there watched from a short distance, some weeping for us but afraid to say anything. All their faces expressed sorrow and some waved or raised their thumb in the air, which gave encouragement to all of us.

After a two hour train ride, we reached our destination, the city of Pech. We were taken to the city prison, which had an attached courthouse. In the prison were many other prisoners waiting for their court appointment. Most of them were there for political reasons like us. Many had already been sentenced and were waiting for transfer to a high security prison usually in Budapest, Hungary's capitol.

We were at the prison two days before our papers were

looked at by a prosecutor. He rejected them saying that there was not enough investigation done in my case because I had been charged with suspicion of espionage activity, and therefore further interrogation was needed. So we were all put back into the hands of the AVH, whose nearest headquarters were in a city called Szombathely, the second most notorious interogation place in the country, after Budapest (Andrasy st 60.)

Torture Chamber

It was 1950 and the middle of February, the coldest month of the year in Hungary. The freezing weather kept the heavy snow on the ground. We were seated on the bottom of a canvas covered military truck rolling toward our incalculable fate. Our bodies were shaking and our teeth were chattering from the cold. We did not have hats on and were still wearing the same clothes we were arrested in.

After a three hour ride, we arrived at the AVH headquarters, a three story building through a large gate to the backyard. Two soldiers ordered us out of the truck, but we were unable to move our bodies which seemed frozen stiff. They grabbed and pulled us out. Then they forced us to stand facing a wall so close that our foreheads touched the brick, our hands behind our back.

They forbade us to talk or even turn our heads and look at each other. The guards watched us constantly for an hour before they ordered us to move. They directed us to the building's basement while kicking us and calling us "fascist," "imperialist," "rebels," and all sorts of names.

It was a relief for us to be in the basement as far as the temperature was concerned. The air was stuffy and it stank, but at least it was warm. There was not enough oxygen there, and I quickly found out why. The whole basement had been modified into about 20 chambers of cells. Each cell had a steel door with a little window in it. Each cell was separated from the other with a heavy concrete wall. One end of the basement was set up the

52

guard's phone booth. The guards immediately separated us by pushing each of us into a different cell. That was the last time for a long time before we saw each other again.

They tossed me into a so-called holding cell where about 15 people were pressed together. The cell was so small that it was impossible to lie down. Everybody was gasping for air. Only a small metal duct in the wall was somehow connected to the outside air without any forced air unit to bring in fresh air. We were different ages and classes of people. Most of them had been caught at the Hungarian-Austrian border while attempting an illegal crossing. Many wanted to leave the country for political reasons. Put simply, they didn't want to live under Communism. Others might have been connected to a spy network. Whatever their reason, everyone kept a low profile. Some of them with bruised faces sat on the concrete floor curled up in agony.

Suddenly the steel door swung open. A ruthless appearing guard stood there looking at a piece of paper in his hand and yelled out a name from it.

A man answered, "Yes".

"Let's go," the guard shouted. "Hurry up!"

After the man left the cell and the guard slammed the door shut and locked it, I asked the man nearest me, "What's going on here?"

"There's a third floor here where an AVH agent tries to extort a confession out of you," he said. "He tries to force you to sign a statement saying that you are a spy for the CIA. If you do, they can hang you within four hours. If he forces you to admit that you are involved in a conspiracy to undermine the Communist regime and the government, and gets you to sign that paper, you will also be eligible for the death penalty. We are all here for

53

some political reason, and we are the enemy. They hate us, and they take drastic measures to somehow liquidate us from society. We'll be lucky if we can manage to survive their torture, first on the third floor and then when it continues here in the basement." He saw how scared I was.

"There is a specially prepared torture chamber here in the basement," he said, "and some of us have been here several weeks in this cell. Some are taken out and never come back, but the cell is always loaded with the new coming in. We've heard many loud shrieks from the other cell, but we never know who the victim was."

I was scared because my case was very serious involving espionage activity, and I would probably be given the death sentence if convicted. All the letters I received from Switzerland were in code, and I was the only one who knew about them. I had kept the secret from everyone, including my friends. I knew I would have to be strong spiritually as well as physically to withstand any torture and to save my life.

I couldn't sleep. I was very hungry and thirsty. I was also physically and mentally tired. But most of all, I was worried about what could happen to me.

Under Agony

In the morning the big steel door swung open again and the guards ordered us out of the cell with a hateful yell. They gave us some kind of soup, about a cupful. One of the guards spit in the soup before they served it. Then they allowed us to use the (so called) lavatory where we could release our waste into a bucket. There also was a cold water faucet where we had about 5 seconds to wash our faces before they pushed us back into the cell.

I was very anxious about what would happen to me. I couldn't sleep that night either. I was so nervous that I curled up on the floor, then into a sitting position with my head between my legs with my eyes closed.

I don't know how much time had passed when a sudden noise shook me and the door swung open. It was still night. The guard's eyes swept over us with a hateful expression and froze on me. He yelled, "You! Get up! Move! Hurry! Get up!"

I got up, and he grabbed me and pulled me out of the cell into the hallway. He kicked the door closed behind him. "Let's go! Move! In front of me!" he yelled, "Don't you stop before the third floor."

He gave me a painful kick to my ankle and after he pushed me to the third floor, he stopped me in front of a door in the hallway. Again, I had to stand facing the wall with my forehead against the wall. He knocked on the door, reported my presence to someone and got permission to enter.

"Let's go," he yelled at me and pushed me into the room. Inside I saw a high ranking officer in uniform sitting behind his desk and at another desk a female secretary working on her typewriter.

The officer was a member of a Special Forces organization, AVH, which was a replica of the Russian KGB. When this officer opened up my file, he was exclusively interested in my connection with the ex-Hungarian political leaders who were in Switzerland. He thought that the letters in his hands were proof that I was a spy, but the letters gave no indication that I was sending political or military information out of my country. Rather, the letters sounded like an ordinary friendship, the writing dealt with family, personal and daily events.

But the officer strongly believed that the letters were written in secret code, so he asked questions about it. I denied that any code existed, and he became very indignant and angry. He threatened to use physical force if I did not confess about the code. He tossed a typed paper to me. It was a statement I was supposed to sign. After I read the paper, I objected and protested. I knew that if I signed it , it would mean my death; within 24 hours I would be hung by rope. So I told him, "The paper is not true! It's a lie, and I won't sign it."

"It seems like you're a very stubborn person," he said. "Well, I'll change your mind in a minute." He jumped up from his chair with an angry red face and yelled, "Take off your clothes and stand on that chair!"

I took my clothes off and stood up naked on the chair, which had been placed in front of an open door. He then told the nearby guard to take care of me. It was obvious that the guard knew what to do and had done it before. He tied my hands behind me with one end of a leather belt then threw the other end over the open door and held on tight. Another guard had shown up by then and he kicked the chair out from under my feet. I was then hanging from the door by my tied arms. Then he approached me with a rubber stick and began beating my kidneys, my stomach and my privates with it. The pain was beyond my capacity to withstand, and I lost consciousness. The next thing I knew I was lying on the floor, my naked body covered with water.

The officer behind the desk demanded that I get up, but after I failed to be able to do so, the guard grabbed me and stood me up. The officer tossed the paper to me again to be signed. "I hope you've changed your mind," he said.

"Not at all," I replied. "What is written on there is not true."

"Well, you are stubborn, aren't you? I'll break you," he screamed at me. "Take him away!" he ordered the guards.

They let me put my clothes on before they dragged me down to the basement. This time they isolated me from the rest and put me in a dark cell alone. I felt beaten and frozen. I curled up in a corner. There was nothing else around me, just the concrete walls and cement floor. My light clothes were soaked with the water that had been poured on me and I felt cold and damp all over. My teeth chattered, and I shook with fear as well as suffering the cold. I was hungry and thirsty. Not giving me anything to eat was part of my punishment, but they gave me something else.

About midnight the door flew open and a guard rushed at me. He started punching me over and over while he howled, "You dirty fascist, imperialist agent. You will rot and die in here!" Then he rushed out and slammed the steel door. I heard other cell doors down the corridor slam, too. I heard human shrieks all night from those cells. Apparently, the guards went from cell to cell all night expressing their hate for us by beating us.

I couldn't sleep. I sat on the cement floor feeling pain all over my body, and for the first time I prayed to God. I asked for help, for courage and strength, both physical and spiritual. I knew I could overcome the suffering with His help no matter what I had to go through. In my prayer and meditation I found peace. My body relaxed. It seemed as though the pain diminished and I fell asleep.

The next morning the door was yanked open, and a guard yelled at me as he pulled me up off the floor and shoved me out of the cell. Another guard carried a container of something he called coffee. He spit into the container and then ladled a spoonful of the liquid into a dish for me to drink. I had no desire to drink his spit, but I was so hungry and thirsty that I drank it. At least it was hot liquid and that was what I cared about.

After I finished the drink I was allowed to wash my face and use the lavatory. Again, I had to finish the whole thing in five minutes. "Let's go! Hurry up!" the guard shouted at me. I had just enough time before they grabbed and pushed me back into my cell. It was so dark in there that I lost my sense of time… of whether it was day or night. It must have been noon when I heard the sound of cell doors slamming as the sound came closer and closer to my cell.

Suddenly my door flew open and the guard stood there with a hateful grin on his face as he yelled "Feeding time!" and threw me a chunk of bread as though he were feeding an animal, laughing as he slammed the door shut again. In the darkness I crawled around on the floor searching for the bread. When I found it, the bread was hard and smelled musty, but I chewed it up very fast.

Again I fell asleep. The next thing I knew I was hit on my

side. It was the guard who had kicked me. He kicked me again and grabbed my arm as he shouted, "Let's go!" and yanked me to my feet. "Move! Get in front of me to the third floor. Hurry up!" He roared as he kicked my ankles. On the third floor he had me face the wall again and reported our presence to the same officer who had interrogated me before.

It was the same room and the officer was sitting at the same desk. He looked at me and said loudly, "Well, well, well! I hope you've changed your mind and will sign the paper, which states that you were an agent for the American C.I.C and sent them military secrets and political information. If you confess, we won't interrogate and harm you any more. If you still resist, we will get rid of you like this." He nodded to the guard who opened the door to the next room.

I saw two soldiers just as they threw another prisoner out the open window to his death on the street pavement below.

"Now do you see? He didn't confess either, and we got rid of him. As you see, we don't care. We count it one less enemy. We don't have to report this to anyone. Of course, he jumped out the window and committed suicide. This is a sample for you. If you don't confess, you will follow him and kiss the pavement, too."

"Why don't you throw me out now?" I told him courageously. "At least I won't have to suffer any more. I will never sign that paper. It is not telling the truth."

Meditated

My attitude made him very angry and he ordered me to take my clothes off. When I was finished he made me lie down on the floor facedown and said, "Now I will fix your obstinacy." His face was grotesque and hateful.

One of the soldiers stood on my back and the other started to beat the soles of my feet with a rubber stick. I shrieked, and they plugged my mouth with my socks. After about ten beatings my soles became numb and I stopped shrieking. Then they lifted me off the floor, stood me on a chair and made me jump down to the floor. It was like jumping on a thousand needles and I started to shriek again. I was made to repeat those jumps several times in a row until I collapsed and fainted. They then packed me in a bed sheet and rolled me down the steps to the basement from the third floor.

On each landing of stairway my body hit the wall. Each time I hit the wall the guard lined me up to the next section and pushed me down with his foot until I rolled into the basement. There he took me out of the sheet and pushed me into the same dark cement cell I had been in.

I was bruised all over. The soles of my feet swelled up and smelled sour. Every part of my body was in pain and I couldn't move. I curled up on the floor. The only part of my body that was working was my mind and I started to pray, focusing my mind on God. I visualized Him as a radiating shiny, shiny, big single eye. I talked to Him and asked for His protection. I asked Him to keep my strength and faith in Him strong. I asked for an Archangel to be with me all of the time rejuvenating me and my soul.

It was a good feeling. I had found God whom I could talk to, a power that wiped out my fear, one that was a companion to me in my dark lonely cell. I had a sudden spark in me spiritually. I felt a strange sensation I had never experienced before. It radiated throughout my body and created a great joy in me. I was so happy feeling God and I murmured, "Thank you, my dear God, thank you." I was so relaxed and calm that I fell asleep.

I don't know how long I slept, but when I woke up I knew I had experienced a beautiful dream about God in which He promised He would be with me, and I would be all right. When I was in the awakened state I had asked God to help, and I had prayed to Him. When I fell asleep, I must have been still with Him and in my dream I received the answer, "Don't be afraid. I will be with you." It was a wonderful feeling. I felt strong spiritually and my fear had diminished.

Another day went by, and then the cell door swung open again, and the guard ordered me out. He pushed me to the third floor again, into the same room where I was tortured and in front of the same officer sitting at his desk waiting for me. I was very relaxed and prepared for the worst, but my mind was with God and I felt encouragement.

"Well, well, well," he said. "This is your last chance to save your life. Sign this paper!!" He tossed it to me.

"Can I read it?" I asked.

"Go ahead," he answered.

I looked over the typed statement, but I didn't notice any difference from the last time. It still stated that I was a spy. I knew if I signed it I would be hung within four hours. I looked him in

61

the eye and said, "I won't sign. It is totally fabricated. You can kill me, but my signature won't be on that paper."

He jumped up and struck the table with his fist. His face turned red from anger as he shouted, "I'll make you die in misery!" Then he told the soldier what to do with me. I thought they would throw me out the window as they had the other prisoner, but instead, he decided to torture me in an even more cruel way.

I had to take my clothes off as before and then the soldier brought in a six inch long by an eighth inch wide hollow glass tube and pushed it into my urethra all the way. He then hit it with a rod, smashing it inside me. When he knew it was broken, he began to pull the pieces out with tweezers… piece by piece. I was bleeding and moaning from the pain when I fainted.

They threw water on me and I regained consciousness, again in agony. They kept pulling the broken glass out which cut the wall inside the urethra. I fainted several more times from the pain. When they had pulled most of the big pieces out, I couldn't get up off the floor, so they wrapped me in the bed sheet as before and rolled me down to the basement again. I was unconscious by this time.

When I opened my eyes I squinted, but I couldn't see anything but the darkness which blanketed me and I wasn't sure whether I was dead or alive. Then I remembered how they had tortured me upstairs and that I was strong enough that they couldn't make me sign the paper. I thanked God for my strength and for saving my life and prayed for further strength.

Refuse to Sign

My whole body trembled, and I was very weak. I couldn't get up from the cement floor. Suddenly my cell door opened and the guard grabbed my arm and lifted me up.

"Can't you stand up? I'll straighten you out in a minute," he said as he dragged me to a different cell which was so shallow that my body just barely squeezed into a standing position and my nose got hit by the door when he slammed it on me.

I couldn't move. I had to stand with my bare feet in water, which came up over my ankles, and every thirty seconds a huge drop of water fell on the top of my head. Each time it dropped it felt like somebody hit my head with a sledge hammer. This was another favorite torturing method of theirs. The guards were fully authorized by their officials to handle the prisoners using the cruelest ways they felt necessary.

I spent about 48 hours in that chamber, so when they opened the door, my body was so stiff that I just fell out onto the corridor's concrete floor and broke my nose. I couldn't get up. My legs were numb. The guard called someone who bandaged my face and nose and massaged my legs to get the circulation back in them. After I managed to stay on my feet, the guard carried me to the end of the corridor and let me sit down on a bench. He brought me a bowl of hot soup to eat. It tasted awful, but I didn't care. I was so hungry that I ate it all in a hurry, but in spite of its heat I was still shaky and frozen.

I had noticed that the guard made a telephone call and reported to someone about my physical condition. I assumed they thought I had broken down physically enough to make a confession, and sure enough, two guards grabbed me and pushed me up to the third floor again.

They miscalculated my condition. They saw my body, but they couldn't calculate my spiritual condition. The fact was I had become stronger inside than I ever had been. I felt that my God had strengthened me and protected me. He promised victory over my enemies. I had no fear anymore, because I felt God's power within me.

I was face to face with the same officer that I had seen before in the same room. He swept his eye over my body. I was so pitiful, with a bandaged face and almost crippled legs that I could hardly stand on my feet. He might have thought that this would be the best time and I would sign the paper for him. He was disappointed when I refused to sign again. I told him he had to compromise the charges against me and modify the statement on the paper. I wasn't an espionage agent and the letters from Switzerland were just friends exchanging letters.

He saw me unbroken, and he couldn't comprehend how I could be so strong and hang on after all those tortures. He became angry and threw the paper to his secretary to make the corrections on the charges. He dictated to her and she typed. The charges were the following:

Two illegal border crossings, undermined the present political system by printing anti-Communist leaflets, agitated people to resist and supposedly, (no evidence to prove),gave sensitive information to the Western Imperialists outside the country. He tossed the modified paper to me to sign. After I had read the charges, I somehow felt released because of the spy issue. So I had hoped that they wouldn't hang me because of those charges. Additionally, God told me in my dream that He would be with me and save my life. All these things flashed through my mind and I decided to sign the paper, and I did.

"You know that we can still hang you?" the officer said. "Get out of here! I don't want to see you again! Only your death certificate! Take him away!" he shouted to the guard.

I was pushed down to the basement again and instead of putting me back in my previous cell, he locked me in a cell I hadn't been in before. There were about twenty people there already. I was weak and hungry, and my body ached all over. I had frostbite on all my toes, and they were swollen. I could hardly walk. The people around me were not familiar to me, but it was good to talk to someone after all the isolation. I had not seen or heard about my five friends since we arrived. I didn't know what happened to them, but they could have been in another cell, too.

I prayed that the torture was over now that I had signed the paper, but I knew that I still faced my trial and my sentence. I closed my eyes and prayed to my God for my future, and thanked Him for protecting me so far. I asked Him to be with me all the time and send me an angel to watch over me in this critical time. "My fate is in your hands, my Lord, and I have faith in your help," I prayed.

I didn't know what would happen to me next. Many thoughts flashed through my mind. I had signed the papers all right, but that didn't mean that I couldn't be executed in the next 24 hours or be sentenced to a long prison term.

Transferred to Budapest

I knew the time had come the next day when the steel door swung open, and the guard called my name and ordered me out into the corridor. I was surprised to see all five of my friends waiting for me to join them. It was a happy feeling to see them again. They seemed sad and exhausted, but otherwise they were in fairly good shape. The guard put handcuffs on us and chained us together. We exchanged a pitiful smile, but at the same time it encouraged us to show a quick thumbs up without the guard seeing it.

With an extra guard, we were led to the backyard where a canvas-covered five ton truck was waiting for us. When we got into the truck, we found about 15 other prisoners already sitting on the truck's floor, chained together. After we were in place, two armed guards closed the canvas on the back, and we were told to bow our heads and warned not to talk to each other. Before we moved out one of the guards gave us a short lecture about trying to escape. "We will shoot you to death," he told us, "You are being transferred to the capitol city, Budapest." Now that we knew our destination, we all knew that it would mean prison.

We sat chained for three hours on the truck's floor in freezing weather before we got to Budapest. It was night time when we arrived. When the truck stopped, we heard a gate open and the truck moved forward and stopped again. When the guard had jumped out he ordered us to get out. When we were all out, we walked to a big building, and once inside, we saw that it was,

Walking the Perimeter
If a prisoner was to simply look up while walking,
he would be put in the chained position

indeed, a prison. After the guards removed our handcuffs and chains, they called our names and told us our cell number.

It was a three story building and each floor had nothing but overcrowded cells on it. Each of us was sent to a different cell. My cell number was 205 and it was about 10 by 8 feet, obviously designed for two persons. Now, ten of us occupied it. We were all prisoners for different political reasons waiting for a court trial. I learned from the others that the court house was located just behind the prison. It was just a matter of time before each of us would go there.

I felt better because I could have some bread every day along with some kind of hot liquid called soup. The sad part for me was that I had lost my friends again. We had been deliberately separated before our trial.

A courtyard inside the prison walls where inmates we made to walk the perimeter, bent over, hands behind their backs, heads down and may God help those who dared to look up.

67

In the cell we didn't have any beds, toilet seat, or water faucet. There were just buckets. Straw sacks on the floor provided our beds at night. During the day we stacked them up against the wall. We had a 10 minute walk every day and each floor went at a different time. We had to walk in a circle, three yards behind each other, with our hands behind our backs and our heads bowed. We were not allowed to look up or talk.

I kept thinking about how I could make contact with my friends before our trial, because the District Attorney would ask each of us questions and I wanted to be sure that we all answered the same way.

One day, when I was taking the walk, I noticed some holes in the wall, pretty deep ones. I decided to make marks above a hole, marks like letters which would spell the secret word "SZILARD" (translated to English it means "rigid") which we had used during our underground activities. Each day when we walked, I managed to make one mark in the wall with a piece of sharp glass that I had found until I had completed the secret word above a hole. I hoped when my friends walked by they would notice the hole and see the word.

A couple of days later I noticed a small paper ball in the hole which I pulled out and hid my pocket. When I got back to my cell, I opened it up; it was a message which read "I got you." I was happy to have communication with my friends again and soon every one of them knew about the hole in the wall which became our mail box.

It was my intention to prepare us for a hearing with the District Attorney before the trial because one of our charges was about finding arsenic poison when my house was searched. It was held as evidence because they said that we wanted to use the poison to kill the Communist leaders of our city. That was a serious charge. So I put a message to each friend in the mailbox telling them to say the poison was for killing rats, not humans.

It was three weeks before I was taken out of my cell and down to the first floor where my friends were waiting. We all knew that were going to have a hearing with the District Attorney, and it was no surprise when the two guards took us to his office.

A red haired man in civilian clothes was waiting for us behind his desk. "One at a time," he instructed the guards. "Make sure they don't talk to each other."

I was the one he wanted to see first. He read the charges against me from the paper I had signed at the earlier interrogation. Among the charges was the poison issue which I immediately protested. "It was meant for the rats. Not for humans," I said.

"But you admitted to it and signed the paper," he said.

"Yes, because they tortured me until I did," I answered.

He immediately threatened me. "I will send you back to where you signed this paper!" he said.

"I will deny it again, because that charge was based on speculation," I answered "it's not true. You can ask my friends. They will say the same thing that I do."

He thought a minute and then called the guards in and asked them if we could have made any contact in prison. The guards told him that we were all locked in separate cells on different floors. "I'm finished with you." He said and sent me back to the waiting room.

Sentenced & Transferred

I watched my friends go into the District Attorney's office one by one and as each returned they managed to give me the "thumbs up" signal. I was proud of them and their courage and solidarity. I had peace of mind as I was returned to my cell and I said a prayerful thank you to my God who had been with us.

A place of execution.
Watching from his cell on the
third floor, Arpad saw as many as
ten prisoners hung every week.

About 10 days later the same guard came to my cell and took me down stairs again. There were my friends, and I could tell they were nervous. I couldn't deny it, I had the same feeling. We all knew that this time it was our trial and our fate was in limbo. I didn't expect anything good from the judge. I was sure my sentence was already decided and that my friends' fate was decided too.

The courthouse was attached to the prison, so the trip took us through iron gates again and into the courtroom. It was a closed-door trial. All six of us were facing the judge and the jury. We had one defense lawyer sent by the court, but in fact, he was only a puppet, who wasn't allowed to defend us at all. I had prepared for our defense in my cell, so I was ready for the trial.

I was the first, and the judge read the charges against me: "Illegally crossed the border twice, caused sedition among the people, revolted, and undermined the present political system by printing and distributing illegal leaflets among the people, a sympathizer of Western enemies, supposedly sent out secret, political and military information to them." Therefore, your sentence is ten years in prison at hard labor.

I had been worried about the charge of attempted murder by poison, but the judge never mentioned it. They had dropped the charge.

I started to make a speech in my defense, but the judge shut me up. The prosecutor appealed to the court for a higher sentence and the appointed defense lawyer appealed for a reduced sentence. Both were denied.

The charges against my friends were Anti-Communist agitators who gave leaflets and encouragement to people who were resisting the government. They each got five years in prison at hard labor.

After the hearing, they put us back in our cells and we were once again separated. A couple of days later I was transferred to a larger prison in Budapest, where I spent three years.

The population of this prison was about 2,000. Most of us were waiting for a higher court decision. Everyone was anxious, including me. The time clock was clicking for everyone. We prayed together every day for each other's fate. I was one of ten prisoners in a small cell. Some of us were taken out and never returned. We knew that the higher court had sentenced them to death, and they were transferred to a death row cell.

The death row cells were in a smaller building in the back yard of the prison. My cell was on the second floor of the main prison, and it had an iron-barred window facing the backyard. I looked out often as I thought about my fellow prisoners who were executed almost every day. I saw them carried out to the death house on stretchers where they were placed in the death house cells waiting their execution. There was a time when I was in one of those cells in chains as a punishment. I was on a different floor, but many times I heard the cell doors opening, usually in early morning, and the prisoner being taken out. He would shout to the last, "God be with you, my brothers in arms. I will die for my country, my faith in God and our freedom!"

I could also see over the high wall to where there was a cemetery outside the prison grounds. I saw people visiting their loved ones' grave and putting fresh flowers on it. It made me sad that the families of the prisoners would not be able to do that. The executions actually took place all over the country. The whole Hungarian country was a prison, so there were many prisons and most of them carried out executions. The prisoners had to die because they believed in God, fought for our freedom and had the courage to stand up for our traditional history.

Prison life was dramatic. Some prisoners were so desolate in suffering from starvation that they attempted to commit suicide by cutting their veins with a piece glass they found or by eating it to get out of the cell and taken to the hospital where they were fed mashed potatoes to push the glass out of their stomachs. That's what they did it for, to fill their stomach at least for a little while. It was very pitiful to see all these things, because some were weak in faith, and broke down easily.

My situation was different. I took advantage of a highly educated fellow prisoner to learn different subjects. For instance, I studied the English language with him, as well as philosophy, psychology, mythology and theology. My mind was always occupied. When I studied, I felt like I in school at that moment, instead of in prison. All my studying had to be done without paper, pencil or book, all of which were forbidden to the prisoners.

I found a piece of sharp pointed glass in the yard during the ten minute walk and I used it as a scriber. I scribed English words on the lime painted walls. I counted seven thousand of them. In connection with theology I studied different kinds of religions, among them Buddhism and Hinduism. From these I learned to relax and meditate. In doing so my soul and my faith in God became stronger and stronger. My optimism in the future hit its highest point. I was able to elevate my soul to an astral level to eliminate my physical pain. For example, the time I was punished in the death row building my hands were chained to my legs while I was in a sitting position for three hours. It was very painful. I was in a group being punished, and some were screaming with pain. I started to meditate and pray. My soul left my body and traveled to a higher level of consciousness. I talked to my God, and He comforted me.

During that time I always had mind awareness of my miserable physical condition, but I didn't feel any pain. The guards noticed that I didn't scream and faint like the others, so they tightened the chains on me, but I still wasn't affected. Finally, they thought I was a "fakir" and they gave up on me. I had sat for three hours in tight chains with the circulation to my hands cut off. They had turned black and it took a long time for them to return to normal.

I had found that a strong faith in God can benefit you. My life completely changed when I prayed and meditated every day. I was spiritually happy, and I always felt a great protection above me. I still do. God sent me a guardian angel as a reward for my faithfulness.

My Visionary
Meditation

Painted in color by Arpad Sardi

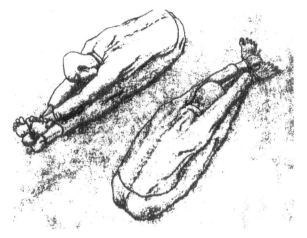

**A form of punishment.
Hands chained to ankles and kept this way
for up to six hours. This torture
treatment was adminstered by the
sadistic guards for just about
any infraction of the rules**

**Waiting for execution that
would come within hours**

Life in a Prison Cell

M y physical activity inside in the cell was very minimal. Ten of us took turns to walk back and forth on the narrow floor space, or make some body stretches. We didn't have a water faucet with a sink, or toilet seat. Instead we had a bowl for washing our face in, two buckets, one for our drinking water, and the second bucket with a lid for our waste deposits. We used a broomstick to sit on, to finish our number one without any privacy. No ventilation, just a small window. We didn't have beds, only straw mattresses, piled up on one side of the room. The straw was never changed for years and became just dust in there. At bedtime we laid them on the floor, creating lots of dust in the air, and we had to breathe them.

Winter time we didn't have heat, so we slept, tight together like herrings in the can, to maintain our bodies' warmth. We couldn't sleep well, because the numerous bedbugs attacked us and sucked our blood.

It is interesting to make a point here, how the bedbugs were operating. Only at night they came out from their hiding place, which were in any cracks in the room's wood floor or in the wall, their flat and brown bodies, the size of a lentil wedged in those cracks. In the darkness they crawled on the wall up to the ceiling, and when they could see a shiny spot below, such as our forehead or arms, they released themselves from the ceiling and landed on our body, as their feeding grounds. As soon as they filled themselves with blood, they returned to the cracks again. If you touched them, they released very stinky odors.

Dealing with bedbugs gave us an opportunity, to amuse ourselves. Because we hardly could sleep, we watched the wall, where they were crawling, and we crushed them with our fingertip right on the wall. In the morning we started to count, how many blood stripes we made. It was a contest among us.

The Execution

In the morning, we creating another dust cloud by restacking the straw mattresses to the wall. Then the guard opened the door, and we put our waste and water bucket in the corridor for the inmates, who carried them away and emptied them out.

Breakfast time. They came with a big container, filled with kind of black liquid called "coffee,: made from roasted oak bark. Then, they gave us forty- decigram bread, as our daily portion. Most of the time, we ate it right away, because we were so hungry.

We could hardly wait until the noon time meal arrived. If we had lentil, or slit pea vegetables, it was a good day for us. Sometimes we had horsemeat stew: cooked horse's organs' such as the lungs, heart, kidneys, liver, from which they made stew.

77

Supposedly we could have a walk once a day in the back-yard, but they skipped that for us, when an execution occurred that day, in the early morning mostly three times a week. If we walked in the backyard, we had to keep up three steps behind each other with our head bowed down. If the guard, (who, stood the middle of the yard with machine- gun) noticed if somebody looked up, he pulled the person out of the line, and after the ten minutes walk, the guard took the person to the AVH commander, and reported the violation. Then, the sadistic commander gave him very severe punishment, such as chaining him by the hands to his legs in sitting position at night- time, outside the cell, in the corridor. Prior to this, they beat him up very badly.

Talking about the sadistic commander we had, often he gave an order to his guards to make raids on everyones cell. What was that all about? The guards opened the cell doors after mid- night, when we were sleeping, and they made everybody get out of the cell, and stood us facing to the wall. Meanwhile, the guards tore up all the straw mattresses and emptied them out to the floor, making heavy dust clouds in the cell, then, they pushed us back to the cell. We couldn't breathe in the dust, just coughed a lot. They gave us five minutes to restore the straw to the bags; meanwhile, they maliciously laughed at us outside.

During the year of 1950, when the Korean-war went on in full scale anytime the Communists suffered casualties in the bat-tle- field, we political prisoners suffered the consequences for it. The sadistic AVH commander practiced his cruelty on us again. He ordered about twenty AVH guards to the base floor to line up parallel, facing each other. Between the two rows of guards was about a six foot distance. Every one of them had some kind of instrument in the hands to beat us with, such as; a belt, a wood-stick, an iron rod, a rubber hose and any different object, which could fatally harm us. Then, we were ordered out of our cell to the downstairs and we had to run between the guards rows, while they started to beat us with whatever they had in their hands, and whereever they could on our upper body. We had to run back and forth, until we all had bloody heads, bruised arms, shoulders and backs. Meanwhile, they roared, "Rotten fascist we hate you." After, they were still not satisfied with their sadism, and they ordered us sit down faces to the wall, then came up behind us and started beating us again. Our blood flowed onto the wall. "Dirty fascist you have to die" they roared. The commander also took part in this torturing; with a whip in his hand, he slashed us. They were hateful, wild and mad. Afterwards, when they saw the bloody wall, they started roaring again, "You messed up the state's property, you dirty pigs? Scrape off with your fingernails you dirty fascists." Then, we started to scrape the blood off, until our fingernails broke off. We just created more blood on the wall. We thought they were going to kill us, but after the furious hateful commander left, we were ordered to move back to our cell. After all, we had plenty of painful sores all over our bodies. The next day, we hardly could move around. Later on, we acknowledged that one of us died in his wounds.

I wrote earlier that I had suffered the punishment, and they put me into that building where the death row prisoners were contained. Here is the story how I got there; at night time, when we prepared to sleep on the floor, we all had a little conversation very quietly with each other, on just about everything. The subject was about a prisoner years ago, who had managed to escape from this prison. Then, a guard outside of the door cells, used a stethoscope listened to our conversation. He thought we wanted to plan an escape. He suddenly opened the door and asked which of us was talking about the escape. I told him innocently, that was only a story, which I had heard of from somebody a long time ago. He dragged me out of the cell right away and took me to the commanders office. I told him I never had any plan or idea about escape. It was only a story about somebody else. Hi didn't believe me, and he pronounced punishment. He ordered guards to separate me from others. They put a heavy chain on me and riveted it on both my ankles; additionally, they chained both my wrists to my legs every second day. The skipped day, they didn't give me any food. The punishment was to wear the heavy chain day and night for a month.

The date was January 1951. It was a very cold month. I was alone in the cell, without any heat. I didn't have any blankets, and I slept on the wooden floor. Physically, I felt very miserable, but spiritually I was strong. I prayed, and my God gave me strength and hope. God listened my prayers. Before I finished my punishment, about three weeks later, the guards rushed to my cell, and carried me outside, where they cut my big chain off from my ankles. They said; I was lucky, because I fell in that group which would be transferred to another prison in the country. I was thankful so much to my LORD for releasing me from the shackles. This thankfulness ran through my mind, with momentarily closed eyes, while they chiseled the rivets off the shackles.

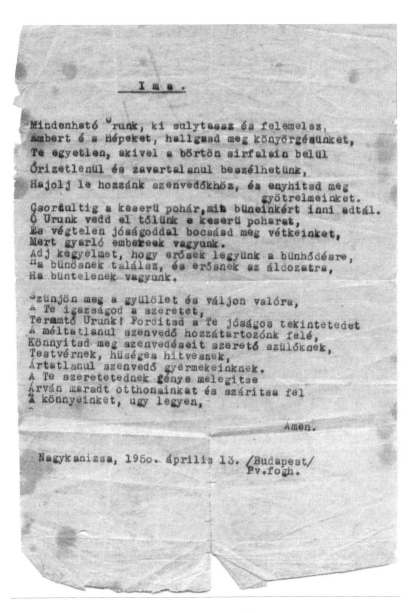

I m a .

Mindenható ^Urunk, ki sulytassz és felemelsz,
Embert é a népeket, hallgasd meg könyörgésünket,
Te egyetlen, akivel a börtön sirfalain belül
Őrizetlenül és zavartalanul beszélhetünk,
Hajolj le hozzánk szenvedőkhöz, és enyhitsd meg
                                    gyötrelmeinket.
Csordultig a keserü pohár,mit büneinkért inni adtál.
Ó Urunk vedd el tőlünk a keserü poharat,
És végtelen jóságoddal bocsásd meg vétkeinket,
Mert gyarló embereek vagyunk.
Adj kegyelmet, hogy erősek legyünk a bünhődésre,
Ha bünösnek találsz, és erősnek az áldozatra,
Ha büntelenek vagyunk.

Szünjön meg a gyülölet és váljon valóra,
A Te igazságod a szeretet,
Teramtő Urunk! Forditsd a Te jóságos tekintetedet
A méltatlanul szenvedő hozzátartozónk felé,
Könnyitsd meg szenvedéseit szerető szülőknek,
Testvérnek, hüséges hitvesnek,
Ártatlanul szenvedő gyermekeinknek.
A Te szeretetednek fénye melegitse
Árván maradt otthonainkat és száritsa fel
A könnyeinket, ugy legyen,

                                    Amen.

Nagykanizsa, 1950. április 13. /Budapest/
                                    Pv.fogh.

The prayer in Hungarian

The evening before we spread our strawsacks on the floor, we were lined up and prayed. Because I was the younger (age of 19) among them in the cell, therefore they chose me to pray every evening.

I want to share the prayer with you which I memorized.

The prayer originally has been written by a Catholic Franciscan priesthood monk, who was also persecuted by the Hungarian K.G.B.(AVH). His fate is unknown. More likely he was tortured to his death or executed. He smuggled the prayer to us to make our spirit stronger to overcome our suffering and to get us closer to God by communication.

The prayer has been written in the Hungarian language, but for the reader's sake I have translated it with my best knowledge into English.

Here is the prayer:

Our Almighty God, who strikes and relieves mankind in Nations, listens to our humbled prayers.

You are the only one, Who we can talk to between these prison walls without any interference.

Come to us and be with us. Relieve our agony.

Our cup has overflowed with bitterness, which we drink for our sins.

O Lord, we are begging, take this bitter filled cup from us and forgive our sins, with Your infinite love and mercy.

If you have found guilt in us, let us be strong enough to cope and repent, and strong enough to sacrifice if You have found us not guilty.

Abolish the hatred in us and let Your righteousness victor upon us.

Our Almighty God give Your merciful love to our undeservedly sufferering loved ones, help our suffering parents, brothers and sisters, faithful wives, undeservedly suffering children.

Let Your loving brightness warm up our desolated homes and dry up our tears.

Amen

Transferred to a Coal Mine

TRANSFERRING TO AN OTHER PRISON.

Five hundred of us were chained up and they loaded us into several canvas-covered five ton trucks and started rolling us out of one of the biggest capital city's prison buildings. The destination was another big prison, located, where the Danube River turns ninety degrees from west to south; there is a city called VA'C. Right at the shore of the river stands a big old building; at one time (before the Communist era) it was a Catholic convent for the nuns. At this point, I would like to note that when the Communist regime took over our country in the year 1949, they eliminated all monasteries, or convents; in the entire country they converted those buildings to prisons, or even to other military purposes.

After we arrived at the prison, they put us into different cells. I was worried a little bit about it; whether they would continue my punishment there, or not. But, a couple of days later I found out, it was not so. Instead, they gave me a job.

Another part of the prison building was set up as a workroom, for splitting Muscovites. Those occur in rock form, to be mined from mountains, where they accumulate in very thin layers. They are generally used to make electrical insulators. Our job was to slit them with a sharp knife, thin like a cigarette paper.

I felt better to be among about thirty fellow prisoners in work, after one month than to be in an isolated cell, wearing heavy chains in the previous prison. Now, I could talk to others, and the days passed by easier.

83

About two weeks later, the situation changed. On a later day, they didn't call me out to work. I couldn't imagine why? It was a scary situation for me. But the same day in the afternoon, suddenly they opened my cell door, and tow guards stood there with some kind of list in their hands. Then, as they looked at me, and asked me if I was well enough to work in a coal mine? After, I answered, "Yes," They marked my name on the list. About fifty of us were selected, and the next day they transferred us from this prison by trucks, to coal mine territory.

The nearby town was called Tatabanya. I had never been in a coal mine before. It was kind of exciting to me. There was a mineshaft with an elevator, which circled around the several wooded barracks. The outskirts of the barracks all around, there stood several machine gun towers, with national special guards.

Well! They unloaded us from the trucks in the yard, and the local commander gave us a long lecture about the camp's regulations and work situation in the coal mine. We were an additional group increasing the already existing prisoners who populated the camp and worked in the coal mine. Each barracks had fifty or more occupants. We had bunk beds. Mine was one of the top ones. The officials supplied us with hardhat and rubber boots, also with battery lanterns. The meals were better than in the prison, because of the hard work. We had three shifts. It meant continuous mining, day and night.

Two barracks made up one group for one shift. About a hundred prisoners were involved in one shift. So, all together three hundred prisoners worked in the coal mine.

Because my vocation was to be a mechanic, they put me in the position, to maintain machinery and equipment in the mine. I was responsible for their smooth operation. I had a bag of tools on my shoulder to carry from place to place, level to level, looking for broken down equipment. Actually, I didn't have to shovel coal. I liked my position, because I could move around all over in the mine; therefore, I had more freedom down there. I had contact with all fellow prisoners, including civil workers; they were the supervisors who handled the operations. My boss also was a civilian, who told me what to do. He was a nice guy and became a good friend of mine.

The mine was very dangerous. Carbon monoxide mixed with oxygen, filled the whole mine, which was located six hundred feet below the surface. Also, tremendous pressure threatened us in the mining chambers. A highly pressurized lake was trapped in and tried to break out from below, and exerted as much pressure by rock layers from above. The mine was so dangerous that no civilian people took chances to work there. Therefore, the Communist government decided to put political prisoners in places like this. Their attitude was if we died in there, they would have just eliminated more enemies.

My position in the mine was very dangerous. In case the mining in a certain location was too dangerous, everybody had to leave the area, but I had to stay back and rescue the machinery out of that place. It really happened one day. The mining chamber got in a tremendous pressure from the top down and from the bottom up. The ten inch in diameter pine beams, which supported the ceiling, broke in half. I was alone in the chamber; I had my battery powered, wet cell lantern and my tool bag. I had just started to disarm a motor drive shaft, when suddenly, lots of small coal, like hail started to shower down on me. I knew this was the time when I had to leave the chamber immediately. So, I dived out like jumping into a swimming pool. Just, when I landed in a safer area, the whole chamber caved in with a big bang like a detonation. I was buried with coal. I lost my lantern, and a total darkness covered me. In that moment I thought I had died, but I still had feeling in my arms and legs. The rubbish coals squeezed my body all around, and I couldn't move. Only my head was out, luckily, and I was breathing heavy. Someone must have heard the big noise and the same time the alert went on. The officials knew where the big noise came from, and also knew that I was working there, and they immediately looked for me. I heard them coming, and yelled my name. "Sardi! Where are you? Are you alive?" I tried to shout back, as loudly as I could, for help. Meanwhile, they arrived at the scene and spotted me with the flashlight. They started to dig me out. I thanked God and them for saving my life. The rescue teams consisted of a guard, one civilian worker, and some fellow prisoners. They told me I was a lucky man.

Coal Mine Experience

I mentioned earlier that my supervisor was a civilian person. His name was Alex. He offered his help to contact my parents, and inform them about my condition and me. I was very happy to hear that offer from Alex. It was a good feeling that there were some people around who had concern and sympathy for us as political prisoners. I was very grateful to him, and I told him, "I hope one day I shall be a free man again, and I will celebrate with you."

As I thought back to that day, Alex took a great risk and jeopardized his own freedom by breaking the AVH regulation: collaboratiion with enemies. The consequence would be five years in prison for him. He didn't care, because he liked me and cared for me, also he hated Communism.

Anyhow, a week later Alex told me, when he came down to the mine, that my parents were very happy to hear about me, after they received his letter. Then, Alex handed over to me a little package and he said; "This is from your parents." I opened it and it was bars of chocolate. I didn't eat chocolate for many years. It was heavenly to taste, as I ate some. I shared with Alex some of it, and the rest I hid in my pocket to save and eat later in my barracks.

I didn't know what happened with Alex, but a day later the officials ordered me to stay in my barrack, that time, when I was usually ready to go to work. I knew, I felt that some bad news was waiting for me. One of the fellow prisoners told me, that one man among us was a fink, and he reported me to the office about my civilian conduct and the small package. Now, I knew, I was in trouble. I was scared. I didn't have to wait too long. One of the guards picked me up and led me to the commanders' office, to a detective. He told me he would transfer me to a prison for punishment, which would mean two weeks in a dark cell, and a one-month separation from the others. (It meant, I'd have to be by myself in a cell for a month.)

I found out who the person was who betrayed me. I knew his name. He was close around me in the mine, and probably he noticed my friendly relationship with Alex. He watched me and more likely also saw the package, which Alex had handed over to me.

Unfortunately, I ended up in a prison, where I had never been before. The name was Maria Nostra. They put me in a totally dark cell for two weeks. It wasn't fun at all. In spite of that, they fed me only every second day. It was an empty cell, no bed or blanket. I slept on the cement floor. The cell was stinky and damp. I did lots of thinking there to pass time, I tore off one of my shirt buttons and threw it on the floor and started to locate it in the darkness. When I found it, I threw it again. That was my amusement. The two weeks in the darkness were like a year. I prayed a lot, and meditated. My mind was somewhat relaxed, because I had given my fate to God a long time ago, and I always felt His protection was upon me. Why I had to suffer a lot, I couldn't answer to myself, but I knew that God knew and comforted me.

After I had lived through the week's dark cell, they let me walk for ten minutes in the backyard. My eyes hurt from the outside brightness for a while, and the tears covered my eyeballs for couple of days; otherwise, I was O.K. I was glad that the worst part was over. Then, they put me in an unoccupied cell, and at that time they gave me regular meals. It was bad enough to be alone in the cell. I couldn't talk to anybody, only to my God.

Three weeks passed by; then some guards opened my cell door. They told me they were going to transfer me to another coal mine, but this time it would be different, from the previous one because I had experience with coal mine machines.

I was happy to hear that. I knew again, that God's hand was in this: God had answered my prayers and got me out there.

The following day, they put me in a truck with some other prisoners, chained together as usual and moved us out. The name of our destination was Cholnok. Another coal mine and not too far, from the previous one, where I had been before. In fact, the whole area in this part of the country was coal mine field's deep-below the earth's surface.

Released From Prison

It was summer time: the year 1954. When we arrived, and after they released us from chains, the official gave us a speech about the regulations. They pointed out if anyone tried to escape, they would be shot to death. Everybody got his own barracks number and bed number.

The barracks were the replica of the previous place, where I had been before. The only difference was that the mineshaft with the elevator was not located in the middle of the camp. We had to walk a mile into a tunnel, in order to reach the vertical shaft elevator to the mine.

Because of my experience, I had back my old position in the mine, as a maintenance mechanic. Everything went well. I met some prisoners in the camp, whom I knew already from the other prison, and we could exchange stories about previous times versus the present prison life and our loved ones at home.

I was very careful this time with prisoners. I learned that someone among us was traitor, a weak character working with the Communist officials as a spy, who was reporting to them, what was going on in the camp, who was breaking the regulations, etc. This certain character was doing those things for his own gains, to get more food, or any kind of favors from the officials. I paid attention to the lesson, and I promised myself to be more careful in the future.

We all worked hard in the mine. Therefore, the officials allowed us to write a post card monthly to our family, but only with a couple of words: "I am O.K. I love you." It was better than nothing. At least our family knew that we were alive and hoped one day our reunion would be for good.

I had another incident this time, in this mine. I almost lost my life. It was a miracle to be alive. God was with me, and again saved my life. I'd like to relate what happened: the mine consisted of different layers of coal, about thirty feet thick. Each layer were separated by about one hundred feet of rock formation. The coal mining had been operated in three layers. All of the three layers were connected with vertical tunnels. The tunnels were only four feet in diameter and thirty feet deep. The tunnel looked like a well, if anybody looked down from above. A ladder had been constructed in there, so, for instance, I could climb in there, up or down, depending on which level called me to make the repair job, or to restored the troubled equipment to operate again. All three levels also had their own slope shaft, where the electric motor pulled up three mine trollies loaded with coal. The motor was equipped with heavy steel rope. The trollies filled with coal, rolled on railways, was directed upwards to level to level, and finally reached the outside ground level.

One of those times when I had a call in the middle level to do some work, I was on the bottom level, I didn't want to use the vertical ladder because it was dangerous, very slippery from the constant water flow. So, I decided to use the slope shaft. Three trollies were ready to go up to the middle level, where my call was. First, I gave a Morse Code up to the operator, as usual; the operator was my fellow prisoner. He got my message, so that I was ready to have a ride up, When he signaled back to me the green light, it meant he acknowledged my coming up. Then, I secured myself on the front of the first trolley, where the steel rope hocked up to it. The distance was about three hundred feet up, on that forty-degree slope. I sat fast on the front. My battery lantern was squeezed between my knees and we started to roll up. The speed was about 35 MPH on the 35- degree angle. It was a narrow slope in the railroad tunnel. The trolley had difficulty rolling on it. On the way, it sometimes it touched the side of the support posts and the top beams. The railroad also was very bad; it made the trolley a shaky ride. What happened when I rode on it, was that the last trolley suddenly jumped out of track, and its wheels rolled on the rails' ties, making it all the trollies shaky and jumpy including the first one, on which I was sitting. Five seconds later, the second trolley jumped out of the track. I was in trouble. I hardly secured myself on the front. I knew, I had to do something. I looked to my right side, for an open area, where I was able jump off from the trolley. I was desperate and scared. God was with me this time too. I saw a clear area and without any hesitation, I jumped between two posts on the side. It was a coal filled dike, high enough, to make me roll back to the railroad with head down, and my head slid deep in, between two railroad ties. In that moment, the third trolley's back wheels just rolled over my head, and punched my head down into the mud. Luckily, it was mud, not solid, otherwise, my head would have been crushed. After a couple of seconds the first trolley jumped out of the tracks, where I was sitting and crashed to the wall. In that point the motor couldn't pull anymore. The operator was petrified above: he thought I had become a pancake against the wall. He rushed down with his lantern and yelled my name, and found me with my head squeezed in between the railroad ties. He pulled me out right away and gave me resuscitation and after I could breathe again. I had almost choked in the mud. "Thank God, you're O.K." he said. I told him, I just jumped off in time before the crash. It was my last accident in the coal mine.

In December of 1955, I was eligible for parole. Out of eight years, I spent six years all together. After, the government looked over my records, they found me eligible for parole.

In January of 1956, the officials notified me that on January 31st I would be set free. They permitted me to write a card to my parents to pick me up.

I cried in happiness. It was a long six years, to be isolated from civilization. I couldn't believe it had happened to me. Yes, God listened to my prayers, and I met with my dreams. I couldn't have been more grateful to God and His Angels, who watched over me always, and so many times saved my life. My faithfulness and commitment to God were secured in my heart forever.

1956 of January 31. That was my day to be set free from prison, and this time from the forced labor camp.

My father arrived at the camp. He brought with him warm clothes and shoes. I hadn't seen my father for years. It was a tearful reunion, with hugs and kisses. I changed my clothes in the guards' headquarters office. They gave me a released document as an I.D. They instructed me that I couldn't leave my own town without permission, and I would have to have a stamped document by the local AVH office in the town once a week. After, I acknowledged the dire instruction, they opened the gate, and let me leave. It was a big moment for me; I felt in heaven. I didn't even look back to the camp, while we walked to the railway station.

I never ran out of conversation, while we were on the train. So many things I wanted to talk about, I thought, are this still a dream? I asked my father in several times, "Is this true, or am I just in the twilight zone?" But my father each time assured me, this was real; I was a free man. I was nervous. I constantly had a feeling that somebody was watching me and I turned my head around. As my father noticed, he comforted me while I had a nervous reaction from my bad prison experiences.

It was late afternoon, when our train arrived in the city station called Gyor. My parents lived here, where I also was born, until four years later, when we moved to countryside. I didn't remember the city, so everything was new to me. My father took the taxi to get to our house. My mother was already waiting for us at the gate. She knew exactly the time of our arrival. It was another tearful welcome, for my mother and me. Six years had passed, sinse I had seen my mother. Anyway, she welcomed me with a delicious dinner on the table with wine. We celebrated my homecoming. I felt like I was in heaven. It was the happiest moment in my life. We also said grace to God, Who made this happy moment possible for us.

I missed my sister, who wasn't able to celebrate with us this time, because she lived in a distant city with her husband and family, but my mother assured me that she would take me to see her.

It was a cold winter. Snow blanketed the whole country. My mother kept me most of the time in the house. She fed me well; she wanted me to be physically strong again. We went shopping to down town. She bought more warm clothes for me, and we took a tour of the town. I liked my city very much. My mother toured with me around the city, we were walking among people, and it was kind of strange to me. Mostly the female persons made me feel big. Six years had passed, I was isolated from them. Surely, they were beautiful to me, the way they dressed and walked etc.

As I walked I always had a strange feeling that somebody was following me, and it made me nervous. During the nighttime sleep, I had nightmares, I would yell, and fight with my enemies, throwing my arms and legs around. These symptoms had followed me also later on in my age.

My parents warned me not to talk politics, because the AVH was watching me. Surely, I was aware of it.

In 1956 February, my mother set a date to meet with my sister, in Hajduszoboszlo, where she lived with her family. I had to go to the AVH office to get my permit, and get my document stamped to leave town. I knew, the secret service was following me, regardless of my permit, but I didn't care.

My father couldn't come with us because he had to work in the textile factory. So, I took the train with my mother. My sister welcomed us at the railway station. It was another happy tearful reunion.

Hajduszoboszlo is a small tourist attraction town known for it's famous mineral hot spring, with indoor and out door pools. I spent two weeks, enjoying the thermal waters in that cold February weather.

During the week, I became acquainted with a girl. Her name was Martha. She was the first girl in my life, and we fell in love. My mother liked her, too. After all, I had a very good time, but it was short. My permit expired, and we had to return to my hometown, where I had to report to the AVH again.

I was very happy to have a girlfriend. I started to exchange love letters, and I was very desperate to see her again. Two months later in April, I invited her to visit our house. My plan was to get engaged to her. She was happy to see me, and she brought her mother over, too. It was a celebration in our house. After all, we were talking about the wedding. We set the time in June in her hometown, Hajduszoboszlo. I was very excited and could hardly wait for the time to come. I couldn't believe I would be a married man.

The time came, and my father had accompanied me to the wedding. The ceremony was in the Catholic Church, and the reception was held in Martha's home. At least three hundred people joined the reception. We had lots of food and drink. Everybody sang in high spirits.

Next day, we packed up and took farewells from everybody and got on the train. I took the train with my wife and headed back to my hometown Gyor.

My mother was waiting for us with another reception in a restaurant, where she was working as a chef. It was a happy celebration.

I couldn't buy or rent a home, so I was forced to live with my wife in my parents' house, at least temporarily. Hopefully, one day we would move out to our private place.

I felt responsible enough to look for a job to help support our family. Martha found a job downtown in a grocery store behind the counter, as service girl. I was hired in the railway wagon manufacturer as a mechanic. Meanwhile, I signed up in college for night school for a semester to study business and administration.

Escape From Hungary after Revolution

In the summer of 1956, a big political event took place in Hungary. The Prme Minister, the same as the Communist party leader, (Rakosi), resigned from his post and he was called back to Russia along with other Russian deposed Hungarian Communist Government figures. The Communism shook his foundation. The people felt that something was going wrong in the government. corruption? Or what? The people used this opportunity to rise up all over the country. So many underground movements they showed themselves openly and without fear started demonstrate and organized against Communism, demanded that the Russian army must leave the country at once. The student of the university in Budapest (Capitol) moved to the parliament building to demonstrate and demanded with twelve points their freedom in the name of the nation. Factory workers in cities were marching out of their work into the streets shouting for freedom, waving the traditional Hungarian red, white, green flags and burning the Communist red one. The people knocked the giant red stars off the top of the tallest building, and they were crushed to pieces on the pavement.

From the factory, where I was working, they organized, and all workers, including myself, marched in groups through the down town streets, shouting slogans; "Go home Russians, we don't want you here in our country." The residents were opening their windows all around, waving Hungarian flags; they cheered

97

us and all sang the Hungarian National Hymn. The Russian tanks moved, but they never used their weapons against us even though Moscow had ordered them to shoot. Those Russians who lived with us since the World War II had sympathy with us. They ignored the Moscow order, and they behaved defensibly. That happened throughout all of the country, where the uprising occurred. The Hungarians fought against Communism openly. The Hungarian police force and the army also stood on the side of the freedom fighters. In Budapest, the AVH attacked the demonstrators, and killed hundreds of people with their machine guns.

The freedom fighters took over the radio station, and we all knew in countryside, what was going on and also sent message to the western free world requesting help.

During that time, I quit work. In fact, nobody was working in the factory. I dedicated myself with the freedom fighters in my hometown. We went to the local prison building to free all political prisoners. We went to the AVH headquarters and forced out uniformed personals from the building with their hands up. Most of them tore their ranks off their shoulders, and gave up without a fight. Then the military took them away and locked them up.

Meanwhile, the fight was on in the Capitol. I decided to help them. My friends and I took a five-ton truck and drove to Austria for some medicine and food. After we made contact with the Red Cross in Austria, close to Vienna, (Austria's Capitol) we loaded our truck with medicines and food. Driving back, we stopped by my hometown. We unloaded some supplies, and kept driving on to Budapest. We stopped at the university and unloaded the rest of food and medicine. They were needed. That time the fight was over. The victory was ours. Many AVH personals and Communist leaders, "big shots" escaped to the neighboring Communist country, saving their life. Some of them didn't have luck to escape in time, and had been caught. They were executed right in the street. Some of them couldn't face the consequences and committed suicide. For example; the judge who sentenced hundreds of innocent persons to death, who, was also my judge, jumped out of the court building's window, ending his bloody life.

I was in Budapest, even after the fight. We burned all Communist books (what ever we could collect) in the city square and pulled the Stalin statue flat to the ground. We were tired and messy. Many of us were wounded or dying. We were mourning, sobbing and celebrating. We were crying to the West, chiefly to the USA to secure our freedom, as Eisenhower had promised us at his election campaign: "I shall support and help all those suffering people, who are behind the "iron curtain" under the Communist dictatorship, etc. We Hungarians trusted Eisenhower. But he disappointed us, he actually betrayed us by sending a telegraph to the Yugoslavian leader, (TITO) that he (Eisenhower) wouldn't interfere the Hungarian revolution. That was what Moscow was waiting for. Krushchev (the soviet leader) withdrew all Russian troops from Hungary because they denied fighting against us; instead, he sent twenty division of Mongolian tanks through Romania to destroy our freedom. He wanted to restore theCommunism in Hungary.

On November 4th, thousands of Russian tanks surrounded Budapest, and at 5am in early morning they started to shell the sleeping city.

The Russians were Mongolians. Their leaders told them they would fight against the American Imperialists at the Suez Canal. So, they were looking for the Suez Canal. They thought the Danube River was the one.

Anyway, the explosives awoke the people. Everybody speedily found out that the Russian were attacking us. We had cleaned

99

up the country from Communism and their followers; now we have to fight against the aggressors, the Russian tanks and ground divisions. Everyone who was able to fight got in their positions in buildings with "Molotov Cocktails" (bottles filled with gasoline and plugged with cotton.) A great preparation began, against a tremendous Russian force. I was also on the defense line. When the Russian tanks rolled into our narrow streets, we began throwing the bottles on them from the top windows. The tanks burst into flame, and they were trapped. Behind the tanks, the ground troops started to shoot us, and we shot back on them. Several Russians lost their lives there. The building protected us from their bullets, and this time we didn't have any casualties. We couldn't hold our positions too long. We ran out of ammunition, and we had to move out. Meanwhile, we heard gun shots all over the city. The Russian tanks were shooting buildings, and their submachine guns noises mixed with the freedom fighters rifles. When smoke was rising to the sky, we knew some Russian tanks burst into flame. The Russians, after heavy fighting finally overpowered us. We didn't have any choice; we had to retreat. We joined with other fighters for a while, until they had to retreat too. The Russians got the victory over us. Their military leaders arrested our revolutionary prime Minister and his associates in the parliament, and killed them later.

I couldn't take the time to make an effort to sneak out of the Russian ring, which was tightened up around Budapest. I was lucky enough to find a way out of the Russian ring. I had hijacked a truck, and I headed to my hometown, Gyor. Gyor still was controlled by the freedom fighters. We heard on the radio that Budapest had fallen and their tanks started to move to west to seal the border to prevent refugees from getting through, or to capture them.

I just waited. I still had a hope that the western countries

100

would help us. My hope failed.

It was mid November 1956. The Russian tanks moved to the Hungarian-Austrian border, and the Communist leaders came back from their hiding places. They restored the police force and started to pick up all those people, who participated in the revolution, all those ex-political prisoners, like myself, and also those who escaped from the prison during the revolution. One policeman, who was friend of mine told me, "Arpi (my nickname) you better leave the country because you are on the death lists. They will pick you up tomorrow and kill you. I didn't have any other choice than to leave the country.

I had a pitiful situation. My wife was not with me that time. She was with her mother in Hajduszoboszlo. I didn't have time to go for her because she was far away, 300 km. from my town, also, we didn't have any possibility for transportation. I told my mother, "If Martha comes back show to her the way west, and I might see her in Austria. Tell her, sorry, I had to save my life and her future."

I said farewell to my father at the factory. He understood my situation and my best decision. I promised as soon I got across the border, I would send a massage by the free Europe Radio Station.

Before, I left the country, I talked to my friend across the street, who had been in prison with me before. His sentence was life in prison and he was set free during the revolution. I told him I had to leave the country, and if he wanted to save his life, to join with me. We could leave together to the free country and built our future. He told me, he had a fianceé, and she didn't want to go, therefore he stuck with her. I tried to convince him, to save his life and to come with me; otherwise, he would be a dead man the next day. After, he had stuck to his own decision, I hugged him aand said goodby.

We had a neighbor, a widow woman, who had two sons, same age as I was. I asked them, if they would like to come with me. They agreed to come with me. I was glad I had company on my long journey.

We picked up the last train, which headed to the border, loaded with refugees. I hoped we would beat the Russian before they sealed the border.

It was a late afternoon on the 22nd of November, when three of us arrived at the nearest town of the Austrian border. Then, we had to go on foot across the field, to get to the border. It was a cold frosty day. The border was a waterway, a canal. The other side of the canal was Austria. We tried to get across the canal on the bridge, but it had been blown up during the war. The water was too cold to swim in and we were running along the shore in hopes that somewhere, somehow we could get through. Meanwhile, we heard in the distance, the Russian tanks shooting wild. (Probably on refugees) The noise was coming closer and closer to us. The bullets whistled above and around us. We thought, this would be the last run in our life, and in just a short time Russian tanks will catch us, and we would be dead.

We almost gave up when a miracle happened. While, we were running and ducking on the shore suddenly, somebody from the Austrian side of the canal shouted to us; "You want to get over?" And we shouted back to him; "Yes we do." It was a desperate situation, because the Russian tank was already behind us, shooting like crazy, and we were just ducking and crawling on the frosty ground. It was five a.m. in the morning, very foggy. The Russian tank hardly saw us sometime because of that, but regardless, his machine gun swept the air in front of it.

Our "Archangel" arrived, just in time. He was a man, who paddled across the canal with a fishing boat to pick us up. As we jumped into the boat, the Russian tank just zoomed by without noticing us. The man saved our lives. We thanked God for sending him for us.

The man, who owned the boat, was also Hungarian. He had a small shed on the Austrian side right beside the canal. He invited us to his shed to warm up. We were very grateful to him. He told us he had already helped hundreds of Hungarians cross the canal. He was proud of it, and we called him, HERO.

After, we spent a couple of hours warming up in the shed; it was early morning before sunrise. Then we took farewell from our friend, and we started to move on across the frozen field, to the nearest Austrian village, which was lighted up in the distance. An hour later we reached the outskirts of the village. As we walked on the frosted field, we found our friends' frozen dead body. We saw him before at the canal and he joined with us for a while, then he panicked by the Russian tank, and he undressed, left his clothes with us and he jumped into the frozen water, telling us to see him later the other side. Surely, we saw him frozen in crawling position on the frosted ground. We felt so sorry for him. He never made it. He was only twenty-five years old. Later, he was buried in the village cemetery.

We got to the village, and then we knocked on the door at the first house we reached. A lady opened the door. And when she realized, who we were, she let us in her house. We apologized for being such an early morning disturbance. "No problem," She said, "probably you are hungry and thirsty." She let us sit down at the kitchen table and served us cookies and hot tea.

After we related to her our war experiences in Hungary, and our hard time amaking it across the border, we told her; we appreciated her hospitality. She wished us lots of luck, and gave blessing upon us to reach our future destination. I have to mention at this point, that the Austrian people were very loving and warmhearted people. They helped the Hungarian refugees a great deal and with great generosity.

We had to move on, seeking a refugee camp. Since I knew Austria, I suggested to my friends, "Let's go to Salzburg." I knew the city before, and I was informed by them that there was a refugee, and distribution camp. In fact the Austrian authorities transferred us to Vienna. There was a major concentration camp and everybody was directed from there to Salzburg. Thousands of refugees were distributed from there to all over the free world, whatever areas the individuals decided to go to.

My friends decided to stay in Europe, so they signed up for Holland. I signed up for USA, since my relative sponsored me already. So, I said goodbye to my friends.

The American authorities set up five buses, with two hundred refugees, (the first group to USA) and transferred us to Munich Germany. There were American military barracks, and we were treated with a great hero's welcome. The Military orchestra greeted us at their gate. Then, after our sleeping quarters had been prepared, the military commander called us down to the dining room to eat.

We stayed two days in the building, Then they loaded us on the buses again, for the Munich airport, where a military transport plane was waiting for us. After we a boarded, we flew through Scotland to New Jersey. Our destination was Camp Kilmer, an old wooded barracks from the World War Two, which served as a refugee concentration center. According to our individual vocation, they would send us any place in the country, where any labor was needed. Because I had relatives in South Bend Indiana, the authorities gave me a train ticket; with five dollars spending money, I boarded the train.

Meanwhile, my relatives had been notified, and they were waiting for me at the railway station in South Bend, Indiana. My dream became a reality. A new world had opened for me; a new life promised a fresh start, with many job opportunities.

Painted in Color by Arpad Sardi

105

My Life in the USA

Iknew the English language already. I had studied it, while I was in prison. My vocabulary got up to seven thousand words, writing and reading them. I didn't have any difficulty taking further education in schools, and updating my trades, in order to fit myself well into this society.

In the year of 1957, I registered in to the De Vry Technical Institute in Chicago and earned my diploma, as an Electronic Technician. I had a new trade as a TV Tech. Meantime; I got my first job, as an electrician in Saint Mary's College in South Bend, Indiana.

During my work, I discovered my greatest hidden talent, which turned my later life into a different perspective of viewing life philosophy, and brought a new enlightenment to my mind.

Here is the story: I saw a chapel in the middle of the college yard. I had a feeling and an urge to go in. As I proceeded, I found myself inside the chapel. As I looked around, my eyes froze on a beautiful pipe organ. In that moment, my mind just disconnected from the real world, and I felt that I was in the twilight zone. I had an urge to sit down and play that organ. I saw the keyboard, and like a magnet it drew me to it. I sat on its bench and as I turned the power on, I put all my ten fingers on the keys. Then, a gospel melody started to ring in my mind, which I learned in my childhood, when I was an altar boy in the Catholic Church in Hungary. I was thrilled. My fingers just pushed the correct keys, along with the melody in my mind. The sounds from the pipe filled the air beautifully. I was so excited because I had never played any musical instrument, or any musical background before, and suddenly I felt like a musician. I just couldn't stop playing one a song, after another. I didn't realize how much time I spent on that organ, when suddenly, I heard a clapping noise behind me, which brought me back to the reality. As I turned my head back, I noticed a nun with a happy face and clapping hands, who shouted: "Bravo! Bravo! It was beautiful." Then, she asked me about the songs that I had played and asked me, which church I had conducted as an organist? I told her I never played before, nor had any musical background, and that this was a new discovery to myself, too. She almost fainted from her astonishment. "It is a miracle! It is Gods gift! This means God loves you and has blessed you with this talent. You have to continue to play because if you refuse His gift, after your discovery, He will take it away from you. When you go home, you must look for an organ and buy one." But Sister, I said. I don't have any money to buy one. "That's o.k. I shall pray for you and you will see, God will provide an organ for you and He will guide you to the place where an organ is waiting for you."

I wondered if it would happen to me. When I went home from work, I told my Aunt about the whole incident with the nun. My aunt also agreed with, what the nun told me, but I asked my aunt, how would be possible to look for an organ without having any money? I have an idea, she said; "Go to the Salvation Army, it is an organization which collects people's donations, all kinds of antiques and used items. They might have in their collection what you are looking for."

My aunt gave me the address of the Salvation Army, and I found the store. I was a skeptic about finding what I wanted, but I believed in God's power, and I knew He loved me, and nothing is impossible without Him. After I entered the store, I talked to a friendly attendant about my request. He thought a little bit, and he said; "I guess we have something in the basement let us go look at it." We went to the basement, and sure enough, he pointed it out for me in the corner, where there was an old antique called Harmonium (organ), made by Hamilton Co. The sound was activated by pumping two paddles. It was dusty, and covered with spider webs, but otherwise, it was in good shape. "I like it," I said, but I was afraid to ask, how much it would cost me? "Seven dollars." He said. I couldn't believe what he said. "My God! It is sold!" I was so happy inside and thought right away of the nun, that God really listened to her prayer, and God had a blessing for me, too. Then, I told the clerk that I didn't have the transportation to take the Harmonium with me. "Don't worry. He said. "We'll deliver to your house; just give me your address." The next day, it was delivered.

I was so happy and also so grateful to God for unlocking my hidden talent for me I promised Him, I will play many of my Lord's Prayers, until the end of my life.

I was playing oftent on that organ, and the music since then became my number one relaxation, even to the present time.

When I left South Bend, for California, I gave my organ to my Aunt Irene.

Since, 1961, I have exchanged organs six times already, as I advance my musical skills. I also became an organist for the Presbyterian Church of Ontario, Ca, for two years.

I was working for the university about a year, when I quit. I switched my job to my original trade, as a Tool & Die maker. My first cousin owned that shop, in Elkhart, Indiana.

A year later, I switched my job again to my other trade, which I had also learned in my old country: a welder. Curtis Wright

Corp. hired me. It was an arc-welding job for the military. I held that job also for a year.

From, the year of 1956, until October 1960, s I lived with my Aunt Irene in South Bend, Indiana. In all those years, I never forgot my wife, Martha, and my newborn baby girl. As I mentioned earlier, I had to leave them in Hungary during the revolution in order to save my own life. I sent money, packages every month for them during three years. I tried to get them out there, first legally, if possible. The Communist government refused to give them passports. So, I didn't have any other choice than to smuggle them out.

I hired a friend of mine, who was a smuggler during that time, at the Hungarian-Austrian border. He went to my wife's house, carrying my personal handwriting letter, to identify him to my wife. He introduced himself, handed over my letter to her and told her to be ready to a journey to Austria with him and from Austria then, legally she would leave for America. He told her more that: "Your husband is waiting for you there with a furnished new home. We won't have any problem, I'll take you and your little daughter across the border; no reason for worry, the road is paved for you."

When, my friend returned to Austria with empty hands, he wrote me a letter about what had happened at Martha's house. Here is the letter: "My dear friend, Arpad. I talked to your wife about the purpose, why I was there. She didn't want to hear about you. She confessed to me that she divorced you three years ago, and she married another man, and she has a child from him, too. She sent the message to you to just forget her; you are free now, to find another woman. My Friend. I was shocked to hear her stories. I still tried to convince her that you were waiting for her and her daughter in the USA. I told her, you had bought a new home and anxiously were waiting for the reunification. "No, I don't want to go!" she also threatened me; if I didn't go away she would call the police. Well, my friend I am really sorry for your disappointment. I did my best for you, but you don't owe me anything. As a friend, always, Steve.

His letter just shook me to the ground and made me cry. I was very desolate for weeks. My relatives had made every effort to comfort me. Since, I left Hungary, I had always taken care of my family. I sent packages, money every month to them. I sent so much money, that she could build a house, just for them to be in comfort. I took care especially for my newborn baby girl, who I had never seen in life before, only in photos. I sent clothes, even a baby-buggy for her. I was positive I would see them one day. I always exchanged letters with her, and her letters were always sounding romantic and she promised me, she would always be faithful to me, and if she will have any chance to leave Hungary, no matter the circumstances, she will leave the country along with my three year old daughter.

It seemed like the promise always remained a promise. She never kept it. She fooled me. She just wanted my money and goods in all those years from me. She thought I'd never be able to bring her out of the Communist country, because I couldn't go back home again as a political fugitive. She thought that Communism would rule the country forever. So, I never found out the truth about her new husband and marriage. She couldn't hold her secrets any more, when my friend discovered the whole truth about her. I thanked my friend, for putting an end to my false hopes and after all, he changed my future fate.

I was lucky, I could get back my deposit money on the house, that I intended to buy. It was a lovely house, with three bedrooms, and was fully furnished in a nice location, in South Bend, Ind. I had to sell all the furniture and appliances. It was a disastrous event in my life. My dream about my marriage just went into the black hole at that time.

I prayed and meditated, seeking the answers from God about my problem and asked guidance about my future fate. One thing I was sure of was that God always protected me in the past and helped me survive hard circumstances, and I gave my faith to His hands, as long, as He wanted me to live. I always pray; "Not my will, Lord, but Thine be done in me and through me." So, I found peace in my mind, Through Jesus, and my optimism toward my future life. I wasn't bitter, or feeling desolate anymore. I told myself; "This is not the end of the world, look forward, build your future; if God is with you, who can be against you?"

I had exchanged letters with my parents during the years and told them, "I shall bring my family out to America." They didn't have any idea, what had gone on with Martha, 300 km away from them. As far they knew, was everything fine, in my relationship with Martha, because I always received harmonious letters from her. I had to write to my parents the truth, the whole story, what had happened with Martha and my friend, when he wanted smuggle her out. The outcome hit me very hard, which lasted a long time, but I got over it and now, I looked ahead for a new future. I want to leave everything behind me, even South Bend with all memories. I decided to go to California for another reason, because I couldn't stand the cold weather in winter and the humidity in summer.'

My parents replied to my letter, how sorry they were for me and how disappointed in Martha, and that they didn't know about it, otherwise they would have of warned me ahead of time, and how they were sick of the whole thing. They also wrote how lucky I was, when I left the country in time because, the next day

111

after I left, the AVH agents were looking for me and searched the whole house in case I was hiding. After, when they had no luck in finding me, they went to cross the street, picked my friend up and killed him.

To respond about my decision that I wanted to go to Southern California, my parents give me an address in Pasadena, Ca. where an elder Hungarian couple lived, whose relatives lived close to my parents' home. They want me to write to them, so that they could help me to settle there.

Move to California

HEADED TO CALIFORNIA.

In October of 1960, I quit my job. I packed my belongings in my car. I said farewell to my aunt, and left Indiana It was my first time to travel across the USA. I had a ' 56 Mercury two door car in top shape, so I didn't have any problem traveling in it.

My destination was Pasadena, Ca. The family's name was Mr. Josef Lanyi and his wife, Matilda. Of course, they knew about my arrival, because I had corresponded with them before I left South Bend. They were happy to welcome me. I was excited to meet them. They had a Spanish style home, on the hill, near the Rose Bowl football stadium. I didn't have any problem finding the place, where Mr. Lanyi (I called him later, "Uncle Joe") lived. He was very nice, treated me like his own son, and his wife Matilda, welcomed me with open heart, and set up the table, ready for dinner. We were talking Hungarian almost inan endless conversation, about my prison life, my freedom fight and my family's tragedy.

I was very tired after my long drive, and Matilda led me to the bedroom, said; "This will be your bedroom, as long you will stay with us. Sleep well." Indeed, I slept into the next day, till noon.

I felt this loving elderly couple, had done everything just to give me in comfort in their home. They took me every Sunday to the Hungarian church in Los Angeles, and many times to the Hungarian Club for dinner, and amusement.

My new life had just begun at Mr. Lanyi's house, but I didn't

113

want to be a free loader; therefore, I was looking for a job. I found an open job opportunity at Johnston Pump Co. in Pasadena. They hired me as a welder. I felt better, because I was able to pay at least something for my food.

I was working for a year with the Company. Meanwhile, I went to school to improve my welding skill with a higher technology. I earned my T.I.G. (tungsten inert gas) welding diploma, which provided for me a higher position, with higher pay. That type of welding method mostly practiced by the government's contracted companies, required USA citizenship.

I was thirty years old, and I missed my married life. I wanted to have a family. So, I was thinking of a woman, who would really love me, and with whom I could share my life.

I knew someone from South Bend. She was a divorced woman. I wrote a letter to her, and I offered her a proposal about a marriage and an invitation to California. A week later, I received a reply letter from her, which indicated her willingness to come and she said she would be happy to see me again. Her name was Rose and her parents were also from Hungarian nationalities. I became acquainted with her at the Hungarian Club in South Bend. We had danced together in party time. Anyway, I was excited to meet her again. She took a bus ride from South Bend. I was waiting for her in Pasadena. She was twenty-seven and very pretty. I strongly felt that she would be my future wife.

I brought her to Mr. Lanyi's house and introduced her to them. They liked her very much. I spent a lovely time with Rose, and we celebrated Christmas together in 1960, and that time I asked her to marry me. We arranged the date of our wedding.

We married on January 7th 1961, in the Chapel Of Roses, Pasadena.

Mr. Lanyi and his wife Matilda arranged our wedding. He was my "best man." The Methodist Minister wedded us together. The reception was set up in the Mr. Lanyi's Spanish residence. It was a very happy wedding. Mr. Lanyi invited several Hungarian families, and some Americans too. We had a happy celebration and we also received many gifts. In fact we needed them. We were poor, but happy.

Later on, Rose found a job at the bank, as a teller. So, we were both working, and earned some income. Then, we decided to rent a house, and we found one. We started a new, private family life.

In 1962, I got my USA citizenship. I was happy, because I could apply for a government contract job, offering better wages. I was seeking a new employer. I found what I wanted. The place was in Azusa, Arrow Space Industries. They hired me for TIG welding. I worked on military projects, such as, torpedoes, surface-to-air missiles, and atomic reactors. Those welding procedures were new to me and very challenging, but I successfully held my position for three years. The problem was with the government job; they laid off workers at the end of the year, when the yearly contract was ended. I was tired of that situation, and I decided to look for another job. Since I had my electronic knowledge, I found a TV technician job at RCA Service Co., City of Monrovia. I was field service man on TV and stereo equipment.

In 1962 February 22, my wife had our first child, a baby girl who was born in Pasadena. We named her Caroline.

I had more responsibility to support my family, although, my wife was still working in the bank, and together, we could share the expenses easier. We bought a new house in Glendora. We owned our first house in our married life. I built a fence around it, landscaped it and even built a swimming pool in the backyard. We enjoyed our home for years and raised our child in it with lots

115

of happiness.

The air quality (smog) in that area later became very bad for me, so we sold the house and moved out. We bought another new home in San Juan Capistrano. (Orange County) The air quality there was excellent, and I didn't have any breathing problems anymore.

I had to switch employers because I had moved. The Sears Co. hired me as a TV tech. in the Santa Ana service center. I was with them for nine years. My wife also found another banking job at the San Juan Capistrano National Bank.

Meanwhile, our daughter grew up and finished high school in San Juan. She married later and got a job at Endevco Co. as a bookkeeper. The company contracted to the Aero-Space Industries, and was located only a half of a mile from our house.

There came a time when I asked my daughter, to keep watch on the bulletin board to see, if the company had any job openings for parts fabrication supervisor, because, I wanted to work close to my home. She promised, to keep her eye on it.

As time went on, Caroline told me about a job opening, at her work place.

I didn't waste my time. I filled out my application and I turned it in. A couple of days later, I got a response to come in for an interview. They hired me as a supervisor in the welding lab.

I was very happy. I bought a "MOPED" motorcycle, which took me only five minutes to get to work.

My job was very challenging. I'd never been a supervisor before; five welders were under my supervision. I knew my welding technique on TIG and Laser weld. I trained my welders, and I had authority to hire or fire them. I had many responsibilities to

116

meet the company procedures. We had confidential work to do. I had to work on all prototype units.

When I successfully achieved my goal, I booked those procedures into the computer for production. My job was stressful enough to trigger a heart condition. In 1991, I went through open-heart surgery, and a triple bypass operation. The operation was successful and since then, I haven't had any more difficulty with my heart.

After my surgery, I felt pretty weak and I decided to leave the company with early retirement.

On March 31st, 1992, I completed my ten years with the company.

In 1996 we sold our San Juan Capistrano home, and moved to San Diego County.

Eight years after my retirement, I decided to work again, just to make myself busy enough to keep my physical and mental condition in good shape. Using my broad technical background, I worked for the Home Depot which hired me in the electrical department part, as I had requested.

After three years of work I had to quit because we moved out San Diego County.

We bought another mobile home in Sun City, Riverside County.

Now, I live here with my wife, Rose, and we are enjoying our old age in harmony, since the day we were married 48 years ago.

We are also happy members of the United Church of Christ in Sun City, California and I sing in their choir.

Arpad & Rose

Looking Back to Hungary after W.W.II. During the Russian Occupancy

Hungary was an exploited colony of the Soviet Union. It started following World War II. In past Hungary was an honor to defend the nation and die for one's country. In the past there was always some area of the country, which was independent and remained Hungarian. From there the subjugated country received encouragement and patriotic heroes. In the past even under the worst suppression, our teachers could still teach our children to love their country and be patriotic. That time, during the Russian occupation they searched for ties with the Soviet Union, and idolized those that sold out their own nation.

Not only is the country subjugated militarily and politically by the Soviet Union, but economically as well. This news also would sound too ugly when spoken outright so a more pretentious name is given in its place such as "Economical Loan and Help Society" (in loose translation). This deception became necessary because during and after the war the Russian totally robbed the country of all of its movable assets. Accidentally(?) they chose such extremely high rates and quotas that there was not even enough seed grain to plant for the next harvest. The livestock was also at a minimal level because of their collection.

The prisons became filled with "saboteurs" of the collection system who couldn't fulfill the high quotas. The market prices jumped to sky-high level, while earning power was kept very minimal, so the farmers were also inevitably

119

thrown into jail.

The (incompetent) Soviet leaders came to the surprising conclusion that it was impossible to totally rob a nation in one year because in the following years there would be nothing left to take. (No way to produce either). As a consequence they came up with a scheme that made the national out-put appear to be constantly growing for the benefit of the Soviet planning commission. This is how the "Economic Loan and Help Society" (K.G.S.T. in Hungarian) came into being. Its basis was no different from the colonial exploitation of the past regardless of whom the occupiers or exploiters were.

The most brutal lie in this system is that for the large volume of food products, heavy and light industrial equipment, and mined products that the Hungarian export to the Russian, they receive "rubles," which they can't use to buy anything. However, these rubles the "great Soviet Union" is unwilling to reconvert to any other currency, therefore all things "sold" to the Soviet Union are actually given away for free.

I must give room for the following information to further prove my point. Unfortunately, many of these short descriptions are but small fragments of the whole picture, which riddle the Communist society.

1) Tractor Factory, used to manufacture very quality farm equipment. The company could no longer export to any other nation except to the Soviet Union. For a while, the Hungarian nation subsidized its losses, but once all of its resources were depleted and even its workers nations subsidized its losses, but once all of its resources were depleted and even its workers couldn't be paid, they were forced to shut down the factory. Three thousand workers went on the streets without a penny in their pocket.

(So much for the Communist workers utopia idea.)

2)   Auto Factory was once one of the largest Hungarian exporters. Their trucks were known worldwide and a special favorite was their 350 diesels. The company had to be closed because it was also in competition with the Russian ZIS and ZIL trucks, and they were unable to sell theirs. These inefficient monsters had to be bought at an exhorbant price instead of buying the Hungarian products.

3)   The Beloianis Communication Technology Company produced communication gear. Its products supplied the Hungarian needs, but it started to export more and more of its products to the Soviet Union. After the modernization of the plant, it started producing materials exclusively for the Soviet Union: secret military gear, computer driven equipment for missile communication. The place was so secret that a person had to have a special passport just to go from one building to other. There were guards at all the entrances. The Hungarian government naturally paid its workers, and I needn't mention that the ordered products didn't bring in a plugged nickel to the Hungarian economy.

4)   Ship Building Company built luxurious cruise ships. For a while no one could find out why these expensive ships were being built for the Soviet Union. (These ships could have competed with the best of Queen Elizabeth English ships.) Yearly

two were built for the Soviet Union. They also built various other ships and tugs. Their exporting at the time to the Soviet only reduced the pay of the Hungarian workers because as I mentioned the Russian paid only rubels and didn't exchange products for rubles.

5) The output of the uranium mines in Hungary previous to 1956 was taken without any payment at all, but following the 1956 revolution Hungary was paid with rubles. In this way they spread the false notion that the Russians are paying for it. Political prisoners were forced to work these mines. Those who were sentenced to prison or those who were "on the way" to being sentenced. This appropriating didn't seem to be obviously stealing until the Hungarian atom reactor was built, which forced the Hungarians to buy back some of the Uranium from Russian at exorbitant prices. How can I accept the notion that I can't eat the fruits from my own garden without buying them back from someone else?

6) After copper was found, in large deposits, the Soviet military immediately appropriated the area and its exploitation promptly began. Again prisons were known in the area. Political prisoners were used as laborers in a very under hard and inhuman circumstances. They lived in so called "death camps".

7) In Bauxite mining, Hungary is at an internationally

recognized leader. However, people weren't allowed to process it themselves. It was mined and prepared and sent to the Soviet Union so that Hungary didn't need to "waste" its electricity for its production. From the Soviet Union they receive the finished aluminum at a murderously high price. Why not sell to the West and manufacture it locally following the improved electric production? One need not think for long about the reason, because Hungary is an exploited colonial country whose purpose is only to be exploited by the Soviet.

8) In 1983, Hungary had fulfilled its potash shipment to the Soviet Union. They took all the potash for free and sold it on the international market, leaving so little for the Hungarians to export that their achieved volume is minimal.

9) Hungary also was rich in coal and coal mining. Some mines had very old black coal, which mostly were processed for chemical purposes. 75% of the coal mines were operated by forced labor political prisoners. Of course, the most coal was shipped to the Soviet Union free in the name of the reparations as usually.

10) The number of military reparations paid to the Soviet Union since the war were raised even after the 1956 revolution. The amounts were so large that the country could never pay it off, and only the interest was paid yearly because the country was "impoverished." One of the interesting features

of the reparations was that the country had to continually pay for all the weapons used by the Soviet troops stationed in Hungary, so that our freedoms could never be won.

11)   In 1983, the Soviet Union removed "its" money from the Hungarian bank. In the party it is a commonly known fact that the Soviet took out "their" money from the Hungarian bank each year. Of the currency earned from foreign trade by Hungarian enterprise, only a portion remained for Hungarian use. The rest had to be handed over to the "friend of the people," so it could have money to pay its spies and demonstrations against world democracies. Even so, the Soviet Union was one of the largest debtor nations in the world even though they have many New York banker friends. How could it have its own money in Hungarian banks (or why could it put it there) when it couldn't supply itself or pay its huge debts?

Let me think back about the valuables which are removed by the Soviet yearly from Hungary. This collection must include the 50% to 60% of the yearly produced foodstuffs; the yearly outlays to support Soviet troops – food, shelter, pay – and to buy their expensive weapons, the annually paid "war reparations." If we multiply this figure by the years of occupation and that again by the many industries which were forced to manufacture goods for them for free, besides the ones which I have already mentioned, then we are astounded by the scale of the exploitation by the "friend of the people." If we divide this cost by the 10 million Hungarian population, then we come to the conclusion that everyone could be a millionaire if the Soviets were off their backs. Instead many persons had no homes and had to lived with parents or friends or whatever dump they could find. Many still are living on the edge of poverty. It is true that those who were able to work independently on a second job were becoming affluent, for they were paid for their work, rather than getting minimal government pay, because their products were not given away for free.

No wonder after all that the Hungarian people were fed up with of the Russian robbery and exploitation. People were in secret grouping underground in conspiracy making anti-Communist leaflets and sabotaging the system with whatever was at their disposal.

The Hungarian Catholic church leader Cardinal Mindszenty, who stood out publicly for the peoples rights, condemned the Communism and its brutality, against Christianity. Communnists were persecuting leaders and destroying the thousand year old Christian traditions.

The Cardinal became the communist AVH number one enemy, so they tried to eliminate him from the society. The AVH arrested him in 1948 December. They tried to brainwash him, and tortured him month after month, but he never gave in. They wanted to kill him, but during the 1956 revolution he escaped and found shelter at the American Embassy. The American government stepped into this matter and influenced the Hungarian government to set him free. So, legally he could leave the country for Vienna,Austria. Later he became ill and died in Vienna in 1975 at the age of 83.

He was a hero and a martyr. He was a paragon of virtue for the Hungarian people; he gave them courage to fight against Communism.

1956 October proved the Hungarian people's desperate opposition. University students organized the first demonstration in Budapest at the front of the parliament building, demanding in 12 points their freedom. The answer was the AVH live bullets. Many demonstrators died instantly and many were wounded. That escalated the hate against the AVH and the Communists and the number of demonstrators became larger and larger, and spread throughout the nation. The Russians over powered our revolution and a new Communist government took place.

According to a government report, 5,000 to 6,000 people were killed; 13,000 were wounded, and 200,000 apartments were destroyed. Nongovernmental sources assert that 40,000 were imprisoned, detained or tortured during and after the revolution by the new Communist leadership of Janos Kadar the mad man who was practicing vengeance against whoever participated or engaged in the freedom fight.

In 1989 a dramatic change occurred in the system in Hungary when Janos Kadar died, and his regime collapsed. A new leadership took over the government,and, from tremendous public pressure, they had to restore the people's rights and their freedom. They abolished the censorship, restored the critics with newspaper opposition. The people could again form new opposition and a political party. So, Hungary today is more liberal democratic than any previously Soviet dominated country. Even Hungary is a member of the NATO organization today.

The reason I include all this information is with the

hope that the reader will have a better understanding of why I involved myself and participated into the anti-Communist activity in my young life.

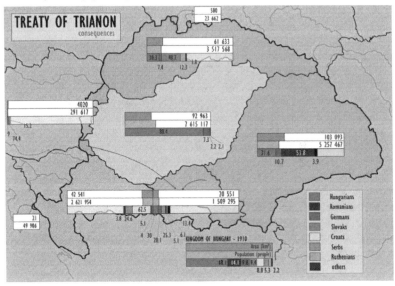

(Hungarian Map after WW1)

The light center area is Hungary today. The surrounding darker area was included as part of Hungary before Word War I

Ed. note: The Treaty of Trianon is the peace treaty signed at the end of World War I by the Allies of World War I, on one side, and Hungary, seen as a successor of Austria-Hungary, on the other. It established the borders of Hungary and regulated its international situation. Hungary lost over two-thirds of its territory, about two-thirds of its inhabitants under the treaty and 3.3 million ethnic Hungarians.The principal beneficiaries of territorial adjustment were Romania, Czechoslovakia, and the Kingdom of Serbs, Croats and Slovenes. The treaty was signed on 4 June 1920 at the Grand Trianon Palace in Versailles, France.

Arpad Sardi, His Story

2648296

Made in the USA